BUILDING A DREAM

The Sara Smith Story

BUILDING A DREAM

The Sara Smith Story

by Kathryn Watterson

Designed by Paul Hoffmann
The Stinehour Press
Manufactured in the United States of America

Library of Congress Catalog Number: 00–090584

ISBN: 0–9678854–0–X

Smith Publishing Group, Inc.
127 El Paseo
Santa Barbara, California 93101

*"I believe that only by having your feet firmly on the ground,
that by way of your love of the stars, your love of great life,
that growth will come to you from within outward. If you
have ever achieved spirituality in your architecture, if
your work ever represented the true spirit of you, the person,
it will be because your feet are firm there and within you has
developed a sense of beauty to be achieved as an innate
sensibility, a sense of what is God."*

—Frank Lloyd Wright, 1952

Table of Contents

*"God's plan is a beautiful plan, and it is a plan
that blesses everyone."*

—Sara Stein Smith, 1997

Chapter 1

MY HAVEN:
Dwelling in a Dream

A TINY WOMAN PAUSES outside and listens to an October wind rustling through the stately oak, pine, willow and juniper trees around the low-slung, angular house that architect Frank Lloyd Wright designed to nestle so perfectly into this hillside.

The woman's blue eyes sparkle and she laughs, thinking of Mr. Wright and the seemingly impossible way that she and her husband met him and got him to design this house. She pictures Wright himself—that giant of 20th century architecture—as he walked through the house in the early 1950s, not long after it had been completed. In his white suit and cape, tapping with his cane on the cypress walls, he studied the way light illuminated the red bricks of the fireplace; he sat and gazed out the floor-to-ceiling glass windows to the marsh in back, where a flock of geese chased one another in the afternoon sunlight.

Wright had designed masterpieces all over the world—from the Johnson Wax headquarters in Wisconsin, to Japan's Great Imperial Hotel and the Guggenheim Museum in New York City—but he looked around at this small structure with a sigh of satisfaction and said, "This is my little gem. This is my little masterpiece."

It still is a masterpiece, built of deep rust-colored cypress, red brick, concrete and glass—materials that speak their own internal language and express a perfectly balanced harmony with nature's landscape. It is the distilled essence of what Wright called "organic architecture"— interior space flowing outward into the surrounding environment.

The serenity, the beauty of this sanctuary wraps itself around the little white-haired elf of a woman, fills her with its playful spirit, its serendipity and magic. She marvels at the wonder of her haven and how its geometric perfection has been woven into the tapestry of her life.

Many times she's been asked: How did it happen? This house has been featured on the covers of magazines and in dozens of architectural books. The renowned landscape architect Thomas D. Church designed the gardens surrounding it. And the famous architectural photographer Balthazar Korab has been capturing its image in every season for the past 30 years. The way that it came into existence seems beyond possibility.

For unlike the Taj Mahal, which was built by royalty, this little architectural wonder was built by people who had no money. They had no status, no connections, no obvious route to the greatest architect of our time.

Both of them were children of Lithuanian immigrants who had gotten off the ship in New York and made their way west to Detroit—her parents initially to Pittsburgh, his straight to Detroit, where they had gone to work, impoverished yet hopeful. Her father sold shoes. His father was a carriage and harness maker. The girl herself had dreamed of becoming a professional actress and the boy of becoming an architect. But instead, both of these children who had known hard times were practical. They went to work as public school teachers in the Detroit school system.

When they started, the pay was two dollars a day. Teaching didn't bring them material wealth, but they found their riches in the work they did, the students they taught, the families they cherished.

And together, they shared a dream—a dream to live in a house designed for them by the great Frank Lloyd Wright. How impossible! They didn't know the man, and no one on the streets where they lived had ever seen him. Also, they were Jewish and no Jews were allowed in the suburban Detroit area where they wanted to build. How could they afford to buy property, let alone imagine living in Bloomfield Hills? Certainly, it wasn't possible. It wasn't even probable.

And yet they staked their future on it.

Of course, their sense of hope had roots, born of a generation that believed anything is possible. After all, they had been born to parents who had *done* the impossible, who had had the courage and the vision to leave their homeland, get on boats and come to America, the land of opportunity. Their parents had learned a new language, a new culture, and made it their own. And even though the streets were *not* paved with gold, they had lived through World War I and the Depression, prospered and raised their children. These children had graduated from college—college in America!—and now they were going out into the world.

This couple, Sara Stein Smith and Melvyn Maxwell Smith, believed what their parents had taught them—that they could and should do good for others. That was their job. It was their generation's responsibility to keep the door of opportunity open for their children and their children's children, for their neighbors and their neighbor's children—strangers or not.

They believed that all they had to do was *listen*—and then pray and work to do what was right to make the world a better place for everyone. A fundamental requirement of living this way was to dream your dreams—and believe in them.

That they didn't have money didn't matter to the determined Melvyn Maxwell Smith. "If you're going to do anything, first of all, money is never a problem," he used to say. "If you have the idea, and if you have the love and the enthusiasm to do it, it's *going to work*."

And Sara Smith's belief in possibilities is still legendary. She always said, "You can do *anything*. You just have to have the confidence to go ahead and do it. Just reach out and *do it*."

Even when people laughed at them, neither of these two young visionaries faltered in their determination someday to live in a haven designed for them by Frank Lloyd Wright. They would overcome the obstacles, and this house would happen. It was only a matter of time.

Much later, an architect standing outside their home in Bloomfield Hills, Michigan, would say, "To do what they did here, the two of them, on this beautiful site—two schoolteachers on the income they had—is unheard of. I mean, it is impossible. Even with all the breaks they got, it's *impossible*."

Feeling the uncanny warmth and happiness emanating from the

house, it's easy to believe that magic was at work here. Against all the odds, Sara and Melvyn Maxwell Smith got their Frank Lloyd Wright house.

Outside of that house on this cool October day, Sara laughs again at the unlikeness of their story. Then she moves slowly but eagerly down the path that leads back inside, back into her place of joy.

"Life is not about what I can get for myself," says Sara, *"but what I can do for my fellow man."*

Chapter 2

CHILDHOOD:
Homemade Plays and Leaf Lettuce Sandwiches

FROM THE TIME SHE WAS SMALL, Sara dreamed of becoming an actress. She and her little sister Thelma—the youngest of Annie Jablonski Stein and Nathan Robert Stein's six children—always entertained their family and guests with singing, dancing and improvised plays.

They were a lively bunch—Minnie, Essie, Helen, Leonard, Sara and Thelma. They had moved from South Fork, Pennsylvania, where Sara was born in 1907, to Johnstown, a suburb of Pittsburgh, where her father, Nathan, was a manufacturer's representative for the Brownie Shoe Company. Both Nathan and his wife, Annie, had been born in Lithuania in the 1880s and had immigrated to the United States with their families when they were very young. Each of their families had been drawn to Pittsburgh, where they joined others from Eastern Europe to pursue the American dream.

Nathan and Annie, deeply religious orthodox Jews, met when they were children, married young, and together created a home that was filled with laughter. Annie's optimism and warmth and Nathan's gregariousness also combined to create a place where their children's friends, as well as their own, always felt welcomed. Nathan traveled a great deal—to Ohio, Indiana, Michigan, Wisconsin and Illinois for the shoe company—but every Friday night when he came home for the weekend, he brought the children coconut bonbons with chocolate, maple and vanilla coverings.

In those days, tiny Sara, with her straight blond hair, large brown eyes and boundless energy, loved to play games with neighborhood children. Running and laughing; kicking a ball down the street that had very little traffic; jumping rope by herself, or with several children using a long rope, Sara always had fun. On the porch, she remembers, she and Thelma could play Ball & Jacks for hours without tiring. They took a break only at lunchtime, when their mother Annie, who was plump and full of good humor and cheer, often served them one of their favorite dishes—potato pancakes. In the evenings, when the younger children—Leonard, Sara and Thelma—were sent off to an early bedtime, the three conspirators would open the transom of their bedroom door and peer over it into the living room, where they could see their affable, social parents and older sisters visiting with their many dinner guests.

Part of the idea of acting, of course, sprang from Sara's curiosity and from her ability to wonder, to imitate, and to pretend. Even as a child, she had the ear and eye of a performer as she listened to and imitated a variety of voices. For instance, when the family moved to Detroit—following the oldest daughter Minnie, who first went there to take a secretarial job for an Army doctor—Sara repeated the way the newsboys hollered, *"Detroit Free Press!"* ("At first, I actually thought this meant that they gave people the papers for free," she says.)

After moving to Detroit and living in a small apartment for a short period of time, the family moved into a brownstone mansion on Canfield, between Cass and Second Avenues. All of the family loved this home. It was large, with three floors and bedrooms for everyone. One of its best features, as far as the children were concerned, was the house next door where their friend James Vernor lived. The senior Vernors just happened to own Vernor's Ginger Ale and had a keg right on the wall with a spigot that turned on—Voila!—for ginger ale. The magic of a faucet that ran ginger ale instead of water was something they never forgot.

In the Canfield Avenue house, Sara and Thelma found their perfect stage setting for performances—a sliding door between the library and the dining room. After dinner, while their parents and guests lingered over dessert in the dining room, the burgeoning young actresses set up their dramatic presentations in the library, and using the sliding door as a curtain, entertained their bemused audiences. They pulled open the "curtain" at the beginning of the play, slid it shut at the end, and opened it again and again for encores. When other children were over, Sara created parts for them as well. "We loved to entertain!" she recalls.

Walking to and from the Irving School where she, Leonard and Thelma went to grammar school, friends remember how Sara kept everyone entertained by spinning stories and songs. And on the third floor of their house, in their playroom, Sara and Thelma often acted for hours on end, pretending they were like their big sisters, Minnie, Essie and Helen, getting dressed and ready to go out to parties and shows with their boyfriends.

Both girls learned a lot about dressing from their sisters—especially Helen, one of the most stylish girls in her high school, who was considered a knockout. How could Helen, as a high school student, dress so stylishly? "Every morning after Minnie left for work, Helen would chose a different outfit from Min's beautiful wardrobe," Sara remembers, "and then she'd carefully put the outfit back in the closet after school. One day, though, my sister Min came home early and Helen was caught. She never went into Min's wardrobe again!"

When Minnie decided to get married, Sara and Thelma, her flower girls, got to dress up for real in white organdy dresses with ruffles that Sara still remembers with pleasure. They preceded Minnie down the elegant curved and winding stairway, around an unusual statue of a lady holding a torch with a light inside of it, which sat at the bottom of the staircase, and into a grand living room where the ceremony was held. "My dress had a blue picot design on the ruffles and Thelma's ruffles had a pink picot design," Sara remembers. "It was a beautiful wedding."

The young actresses were not without a more practical side. They planted a vegetable garden—and grew lettuce. "We would go into the house and get bread with butter and bring it out to our garden," says Sara. "We put the leaf lettuce in between the bread and made the *best* lettuce sandwich you can imagine."

Sara's dreams of acting never wavered. When the Stein family moved from the home on Canfield Avenue, which became too expensive to maintain, to a smaller home on Alger Avenue, Sara met and became great friends with Sara Horowitz, who lived next door and also loved acting and actors. "Sara was like a sister to me," Sara Horowitz Levine remembered from her home in Detroit some 80 years later. "I was the only child in my family, and since my mother and father had a grocery store, and my mother always helped my father, I was alone a lot. But every time I went to the Stein's, there were so many people! They were just a wonderful family! It practically became my second home.

"I loved going there, and I loved being with Sara. She was always laughing, always fun — just a grand person. She was a talker — and she made friends with everybody. Everybody! She's got so many friends, she always has. She introduced me to her friends and took me everywhere. Even as a kid, she always had children with her. She used to say, 'We're all God's children,' and she seemed to love everybody. When she went to camp in the summers, she insisted I go with her, but since I was the only child, my parents worried, and so I didn't go with her. But I was with her again when she came home.

"Sara always was very close to her mother. She was always doing the dishes for her. When I came there, Sara would wash and I would dry the dishes. Sara's mother was so gracious and so nice. She enjoyed playing poker—and she used to say that it was okay because only anything over a penny is gambling."

Sara, Thelma and "Sari," as Sara Horowitz was called to keep the two Saras straight, used to go to the cinema on Saturdays to watch Charlie Chaplin, Douglas Fairbanks, Mary Pickford, Cecil B. De Mille, Buster Keaton, Greta Garbo and other favorites. Just as children trade baseball cards today, the girls then traded pictures of actors and actresses that they cut from magazines and newspapers. "Sara always talked about acting, and she loved going to the movies and exchanging photographs of the actors and actresses," Sara Horowitz recalls.

After high school, when adored big brother Leonard was studying at the University of Michigan, it was time for Sara's first real step towards the stage. "I made arrangements to go to Carnegie Tech in Pittsburgh," says Sara. "I did so want to become a professional actress, and they had a wonderful drama program there. But when my family heard me saying I wanted to be a professional actress, they said, 'No, no, no. We won't have an actress in the family.' At that time, acting was not considered a refined career," she says. "It was the early 1920s, and in those days, acting was thought to be degrading. My parents wouldn't consider letting me be a professional actress.

"I was a good girl," she says simply. "I wouldn't go against their wishes. Also, they were the ones paying for me to go to college. So I went to Ypsilanti, which is now known as Eastern Michigan University, and I studied to become an early elementary teacher."

Her time at Ypsilanti opened the world for Sara in several ways. First, she was exposed to new foods. At home, Sara had followed kosher dietary laws, and had never eaten meat with dairy. "Being Jewish, I had tried not to eat meat at dinner," she says, "but one night the girl next to me was served a lamb chop, and I thought, 'Oh, what the heck, I'm going to get a regular meal.' So I told the waitress, 'I'll have the regular meal.' She brought it to me, and I had cut it and was ready to put it in my mouth when the girl next to me said, 'Oh, this pork chop is absolutely delicious.' When I heard 'pork,' I put down my fork. I just couldn't eat that food."

Another change Sara faced was the reality of working. Though neither Leonard, who was up in Ann Arbor, nor Sara had ever worked, Sara's new roommate had a job, as did other girls she met. "I thought, Gee, if they work, why can't I?" She got a job in the college cafeteria—emptying dishes from the dishwasher—that launched her working life. She worked there all the way through college in exchange for three free meals a day.

In Ypsilanti, Sara also ran into bigotry. At the end of her first semester, she needed a new roommate for the spring, and she met a girl she liked a lot. "I hadn't mentioned anything about needing a roommate," she says. "But as we were strolling along, she started telling me about a little cousin who lived in Ypsilanti. The mother of this child had gone shopping for a pair of pants and found a bargain. When she brought her purchase home, she found that one pant leg was shorter than the other. She said she'd purchased the pants at a Jewish store. The girl then said, 'I told her, What can you expect from Jews?!'

"'Well,' thought I, 'there goes my possible roommate!'"

After that, Sara persuaded her friend and neighbor from home—Sara Horowitz—to come to Ypsilanti to be her roommate. Their friendship had never faltered, and it didn't falter now. The two Saras loved being together in college. They shared everything—including treats from Sari's father's grocery story. When Sari used to come back from weekends at home, she always came laden with groceries. Besides the cookies and candy, Sara's favorite treat was Ritz crackers spread with peanut butter.

"Oh, I remember those delicious crackers with peanut butter," Sara says some 70 years later, closing her eyes and savoring the remembered taste with a genuine, child-like gladness. "How wonderful it was!"

"Talk to God before you talk to man," says Sara.

Chapter 3

AND SO IT BEGINS:
The Early Days of Theater

IN HER INIMITABLE WAY, Sara threw herself wholeheartedly into her studies. Majoring in early childhood education, she was a good student, and she looked forward to becoming a kindergarten teacher. But she never gave up her acting dream. All of the time she was in college, she *knew* that somehow, some way, when she began to earn her own money, she would act on stage and stay connected to the theater.

Sara was the first person in her family to earn a college degree, which was a matter of great pride for her sisters and parents, and she wasn't about to let them down. After graduating from Ypsilanti, she applied for a teaching job in Detroit. "This was Depression times, and all they offered was to put me on the substitute list," she says. "I was quite insulted to think that they didn't assign me a teaching position right away. So instead I got a job at a department store, Crowley Milner's, earning a dollar a day. My mother said, 'Sara, why don't you try to substitute for one day?' So I did, and I loved it. The principal asked me to come back the next day. And I earned seven dollars a day! I quit my job at Crowley Milner's and substituted, and I got called almost every day. At one school I went to, Esterbrook, the principal—Miss Vendenberg—liked me and asked that I be given a permanent substitute job at her school. So, before you know it, I was given a job at that school as a regular teacher."

As soon as she started to teach and was earning her own money, however, Sara also enrolled as an evening student at the Jessie Bonstelle Theatre School in Detroit. At the beginning, she studied with Olga

Tricher, who ran the school and taught all phases of the theater. Then Tricher moved the school and most all of its teachers to New York. Only one teacher from the school stayed on in Detroit, and that was Madame Rebora, a speech and drama teacher who moved her classes to the Wardell Apartment Hotel. For five years, Sara went to the Wardell Hotel every Saturday morning to study with Madame Rebora. "She taught me the Italian method of breathing, which has been so very helpful, even now," says Sara. "She was great on diction, improvisation, everything. She had me memorize many selections from Shakespeare and from other great literary works. I realize now, in retrospect, that she could see that I had talent. She always worked overtime with me, and I learned so much working with her.

"Later, when Madame Rebora retired, she gave me her collection of plays and other theater materials she used in teaching. She was a wonderful lady and a devoted teacher. I will never forget her. Eventually, I gave most of the materials to my daughter-in-law, thereby passing it on, in a direct sense, to the next generation."

Sara cherished her acting dream. "At 3:30 every day, after I finished my teaching, I became an actress," she says. "I joined several theater groups and performed in many plays with them—some for a little pay and some for free. I had a great time, and then I finally was accepted at Wayne State University Theater. The director, Richard Dunham, was wonderful. The school had very little money to give the drama department, but Richard Dunham was an absolute professional. He was a great director, just a genius in lighting, and he could create all kinds of wonderful effects on stage.

The first play Sara was in was *The Daughters of Atrius*. She played the part of the nurse—a good character part—and her whole family and all of her friends came to see the play. "They were just so thrilled, and of course I was, too, because that was the beginning of my acting career," says Sara. "When I got home from that opening night, they had stars all over the door of my bedroom and in my bedroom itself! It was wonderful."

Some of the other shows Sara acted in at the Wayne State University Theater were *Six Characters in Search of an Author*; Congreve's *Way of the World*; *Our Town*; and *Abraham Lincoln*, in which she was Aunt Polly.

("I loved the long dress, the bonnet, the high topped shoes.") "In Congreve's *World,* I was a barmaid, and I made one entrance and ran into the arms of a nobleman. As I was about to say my line, my mind went completely blank. However, the young man who caught me ad-libbed until I remembered my lines. That had never happened to me before, and it scared me so much I thought I would never want to act again. Everything from then on went smoothly, though, and I learned that when you are patient, your needs are always met.

Sara's niece, Phyllis Clinton, Minnie's youngest daughter, remembers Sara's acting with great pleasure. At the time, they all lived together in the Stein house, where Minnie had returned to live with her two daughters, Phyllis and Elaine, and her husband, who was very ill with rheumatoid arthritis. From the time she was about five years old until she was 14, Philly, along with her older sister Elaine, shared Sara and Thelma's room. It was a big bedroom with two double beds—one for Philly and Elaine, one for Sara and Thelma. "When Elaine and I were little, Thelma and Sara would come home from their dates, and talk and giggle," Philly recalls. "They were like two peas in a pod, they were so close. All the sisters were close, but they were like twins. Elaine and I would be sleeping, but sometimes I would wake up and listen. One night, they put a slip over the lampshade so it wouldn't wake us up, and the slip caught on fire. It was pretty exciting.

"Sara was like a second mother to me when I was young," Philly says. "My mother was so busy with a sick husband and full-time work that I sort of looked to Sara as my mother figure. As I got older, I could relate to my mother more, but when I was young, Sara was it. She was so fun-loving and so kind. She'd plan trips for me on Saturday mornings. She took me through *The Detroit News,* where they showed you how the newspaper was put together, and to the WJR radio station, and other places like that. Oh, I counted on her so much.

"She loved the theater, and she loved acting. Everything she said and did was very theatrical. She just emulated everything that was good in life. I used to rehearse with her. I would read the lines to her so that she could practice and come in with her lines. I remember when she was in *Our Town* and we practiced and practiced. . . ."

Sara used to invite the principal of the school where she was teaching to come and see her performances. Miss Vendenberg told her, "You're not a kindergarten teacher! You should be a performing arts teacher!" A few years later, she *was* promoted to the Performing Arts Department . . . but not until she'd had a number of other teaching experiences.

In December, 1936, Sara joined a theater group that was putting on *Lady Windermere's Fan* and got the part of the Dutchess. "It was a great part," Sara recalls. "And it gave me the opportunity to use my English accent. I loved the character." The group performing *Lady Windermere's Fan* worked under the direction of a woman named Helen Howard from the Detroit radio station WXYZ. "Henry Ford had given a grant to the station to be used in the arts, and that was financing Helen's work with our theater group," Sara says. "That spring, we met two evenings a week and worked on the show. Then Helen asked me if I would like to work for the 12 o'clock radio news program Monday through Friday in Windsor that summer. I wouldn't receive a salary, but I would have transportation, lunch and the experience. This was the type of work I had dreamed about doing."

At the same time, however, Sara received a call from the Jewish Community Center asking her to work for them as a counselor at their Fresh Air camp in Brighton, which catered to underprivileged children as well as to children who paid full tuition. That previous summer, Sara's cousin, Sidney Moyer, who was working as a drama coach at a nearby camp, had called her and asked her to fill in for a counselor who had had to go home on emergency leave. Sara had worked in the camp nursery through the remainder of the summer, and because she thoroughly enjoyed the experience, she had placed her name at the Jewish Community Center, saying she would be interested in the Fresh Air camp. But now that she had the radio offer as well, she was in a quandary.

"I told them that now I was not interested in doing the camp work," she says. "But they were quite persistent, and they continued calling. I told them again and again I wasn't interested, but I started to hear a little voice inside that seemed to say, 'Go to camp!' But I did not *want* to go to camp. I wanted to work at that radio station in Windsor. It was quite a mental battle. I finally talked to Helen Howard about it. Helen said I could keep my part in *Lady Windermere's Fan* if I could come to Detroit once a week. I knew I could do that because the camp gave its counselors 24-hour leave once a week, and Brighton was only a little over an hour's ride from Detroit.

"Well, the camp won out. And it's interesting that, ultimately, my decision to accept the camp job eventually led to meeting my husband."

At the Fresh Air camp during the summer of 1936, Sara was head counselor, which meant she worked from 7 a.m. to 11 p.m. Two hundred children came to the camp to be in the country for two- and three-week periods. Sara was in charge of a dorm, which had two wings that each housed 25 campers and six counselors.

"I enjoyed it, especially the younger children," Sara recalls. "The camp didn't have money to buy any equipment for the little ones. The kitchen had box crates of all sizes and a lot of interesting materials that they usually threw away. So we used these materials to make trains and little towns and all kinds of buildings. It was exciting to watch the children work and create."

Younger counselors appreciated Sara's quick laugh and her spontaneity and warmth as much as the children did. "That summer was my first experience as a counselor, and I was very fortunate that Sara was head counselor," Annie Aptekar remembers. "She was a little older, but she was able to relate to the younger women who were there on our level. She never made us feel uncomfortable. She was very considerate of our feelings, and I think that's a word—considerate—that describes Sara very well. And I think it's because of her philosophy of life. She just loves everyone and sees only good in everyone.

"After that summer, I was an arts and crafts counselor at two different camps—one a Jewish Community Center day camp and later one in Grosse Pointe. But I never met anyone like Sara. Sara was unique."

Annie wasn't the only one who saw Sara's special talents. At the end of the summer, the director of the camp, Irwin Shaw, apologetically handed Sara a check for $25.00—her salary for the summer.

"You don't need to apologize," Sara said. "That was the amount I was expecting."

"Of course you will be back next summer?" he asked.

"No, I won't be returning," she answered.

"What if I can offer you something better?" he said. "I really want you back at camp next summer. It wouldn't be the same without you!"

During that school year, Sara taught her classes, and after 3:30 p.m., performed with a theater group several days a week. She also worked at a theater school for a young man named Saul Schlesinger. One day in the spring, Saul asked Sara if she would help him with a summer theater program for children. As they were sitting talking about how to organize the summer program, the director of the Fresh Air camp, Irwin Shaw, walked in and said, "Sara! I want you to be my assistant director this summer! I just found out that the former assistant director is not coming back, and I want you to be my assistant director for the girls."

"Sara isn't going to work for you this summer," Saul Schlesinger said. "She is going to work for me, aren't you, Sara?"

"No she's not. She's working for me," Irwin Shaw argued. "Sara, I'll be able to give you a salary of $250 for the summer."

"Wait a minute, you two," Sara interrupted. "I will make the decision about what I'm going to do, and I will let you know my answer."

"There was no question about Sara," Irwin Shaw said years later. "I had spotted somebody who was great with children, and I wanted to have her at camp. I don't know how I adjusted the budget, but I knew I wanted her there. What was special about Sara was so obvious. She was such a loving person, so giving and concerned, always ready to be helpful. The thing that caught your fancy was the fact that she was very warm and was so interested in other people. It was so apparent. And when you're looking for people who are going to take care of children, you can't help but notice her. You felt a sense of trust that if Sara was there, things would be done properly."

After a day or two of thinking, Sara accepted the camp job. Being an assistant director and administrator at the camp appealed to her. And, the summer of 1937 at Fresh Air was, as Irwin Shaw had promised, a "brand new ball game." Sara found that in her new job she could have a lot of fun and the freedom to be creative without having to be part of a formal dramatic organization. As assistant director for the girls, she also had her own private quarters and ten times the pay of the previous summer. But one of the best things about that summer was meeting Irv Rosen, who was assistant director for the boys.

"Irv Rosen and I worked so well together," Sara says. "We planned meals for the camp, supervised all the activities. On rainy days, when all the children had to stay indoors, Irv and I would put on shows in the recreation room for the whole camp. Since the two of us were both theater people, we had the talent to entertain the campers—and they loved it."

"Sara and I had instant rapport," Rosen says, chuckling at his memories. "We got along like we were brother and sister. I'll tell you one thing. Sara never saw a bad child at the camp; every child was good. She never saw a bad person in her life. And she really felt that way. And it was just part of her personality to believe that everybody is wonderful. Everybody has something to offer. It was just part of her makeup."

"We put on one play—an old-fashioned one, set in the 1800s, that we got from a music sheet that Sara brought in. We made up a stage setting and old-fashioned costumes. She was sitting on a bench in the park (on stage), and I came along and I sang, 'Tell me, pretty maiden, are there any more at home like you?' And she answered, 'There are a few, kind sir, but simple girls are wonderful, too!'"

Sara and Irv often sat around a campfire late in the evenings, telling the campers stories. One story featured a famous Indian who had lived in that area of Michigan, not far from the Fresh Air camp, a long, long time ago. Sometimes the ghost of this Indian, Minutonka, still talked at night, and Irv would tell the children, "If you're very quiet and you listen hard, sometimes you still can hear Minutonka talking." He would call, "Are you there, Minutonka?" Then, out of the night air and the darkness of the woods, a voice would sing: "I am here, loving all the children of Fresh Air camp."

The children would sit with their mouths open as they heard this Indian speaking. Then Sara would talk about a princess, Mekonka, who, like Minutonka, was part of this Indian group. She would tell a story about Mekonka, and then she'd say, "Now everybody be quiet, and we'll see if the ghost of Mekonka will answer." She'd call out, "Are you there, Mekonka?" And a woman's voice would answer, "I am here! And I love all the people from Fresh Air camp."

At the end of the summer, Irwin Shaw asked Sara if she would come teach at his Sunday school. Despite the fact that Shaw was barely out of college, he had gotten married and had been appointed to his first teaching position. He also had become the principal of the Sunday school at B'nai Moshe, a synagogue not far from the Stein's home. He had a knack for putting good people—people genuinely interested in children—together, and he knew Sara would add her lively energy, dedication and laughter to his teaching faculty.

Sara, who had been losing interest in Judaism and straying away from synagogue services as well, wasn't sure she wanted to get involved. When she mentioned it to her parents, however, they were delighted. Both were getting a little worried about Sara's prospects for marriage. She had dated a number of men, but no one seemed to stick, and teaching at the synagogue school couldn't help but open her options. "My mom was so thrilled that I thought, well if it will please my mother that much, maybe I should do it," Sara says. "Of course she was so enthused because I would be meeting people of my own faith. She said to me, 'Maybe you might even meet a nice Jewish boy!' So, to please my parents, I said yes to Mr. Shaw and accepted the teaching job."

"Love is the key to everything," says Sara. "So we must love everyone and everything."

Chapter 4

CHANGES:
Early Love and Loss

SARA WAS AS BIG A HIT at the Sunday school as she was at camp. "She was always doing dramatics at the school, and you could not *not* be drawn to her," her friend Lil Chinitz remembers. "When she talked to you, she would look you right in the eyes and smile, and you just had to love her right away."

Ben Chinitz, who eventually replaced Irwin Shaw as Sunday school principal, remembers Sara's ability to bring out the best in every child. "I used to watch Sara when she taught the youngsters, and she was really a magician," he says. "She was like somebody who works with puppets. She'd pull a string and get a reaction. Whether it was the little ones or the kids of high school age, whenever she worked with them in the area of drama, it was simply mesmerizing. Teaching Sunday school for adolescents is not an easy thing. When she worked out dramatic presentations, the kids would come in extra during the week to work with her."

During this time, Sara also was performing on stage. But then, two heartbreaking, and ultimately life-changing, events sunk her into a deep depression. One was a love affair that didn't pan out. The other was the greatest tragedy of her life: the disappearance of her big brother Leonard.

"Leonard was brilliant," Sara remembers. "And he was beautiful, so beautiful. He was a wonderful tennis player and a wonderful piano player. He was so gifted in music that the nuns who taught him used to say, 'Someday we'll hear from him because he's so talented.' Leonard also was a writer, a very very good writer. He used to ride box cars just to get experiences to write about. Oh, he loved to write."

Phyllis Clinton remembers the intensity of Leonard's desire to write. "We lived in this big apartment, and Leonard would always yell at us because we made noise when he was trying to write," she says. "He was working on his stories. And we were playing. So he was always writing, and he was always yelling, 'Will you kids keep quiet!'

"My grandmother adored him. He was the apple of her eye, her favorite child, I think. But finally he told my grandmother that he just couldn't write from home or from Ann Arbor. He said that he had to go to New York to be a writer."

And so it was that only a short time before he was supposed to graduate from the University of Michigan, Leonard Stein left Ann Arbor and headed for the bohemian lifestyle of New York. For the rest of the family it seemed as if Leonard's departure was sudden, unexpected. "He just left," Sara remembers. "He only had a few months to graduate. But he wanted to go to New York to write. He had written a book that he took with him to finish. When Leonard left, he said, 'If I succeed, you will hear from me.'"

Nathan and Annie Stein were very upset with their only son. Upset, angry, disappointed and frustrated. It was almost beyond their comprehension. Why, when he was so close to graduation, wouldn't he stay to graduate? Why did he have to go to New York? Why did he have to be a writer? How could he leave his mother like that? How could he disobey their wishes on what seemed to be a whim? Also, when he had what for them was an extraordinary, almost unbelievable opportunity—a chance to graduate from college in America, to be secure, to ensure his future—*why, why, why* would he turn it down?

"My parents were not at all pleased with Leonard, and they refused to support him unless he finished college," Sara says. Leonard and Sara corresponded, but she never shared his letters with the family. "I always used to write to him and I sent him money from my teaching salary."

But the time came when Sara received a letter from Leonard asking her for some more money, and she didn't send what he asked. She didn't send anything at all. It was the only time she had failed to send him money when he asked for it. Then, as time went on, no more letters came from Leonard. All of a sudden, Sara realized, the letters had stopped coming. She wrote to him again and again without getting any response. Sara, his closest correspondent and closest sibling, never got another word from him. Nor did anyone else.

No one heard anything. No one could find out anything.

They never could find Leonard. He was nowhere to be found.

Helen hired a detective to follow his trail. But the detective came up with nothing. And when Sara's mother and father sent Helen and Essie to New York to look for him, they didn't find any clues to follow.

"I have my own thoughts about it," says Philly. "I used to tell Thelma and Sara, and they thought I was nuts. But when you love someone, you think of him as an angel, even if he has faults. I think he went to New York and got into serious trouble and couldn't find a way out. That's my own opinion. It was tragic."

But whether Leonard just couldn't cope or found himself in serious trouble will probably never be known. He just disappeared off the face of the earth without a trace. Sara agonized over the fact that she hadn't sent him money the last time he had asked for it, but there was no way to turn back time. Nobody ever saw Leonard again.

Besides her grief about Leonard, Sara's heart also was broken by a love affair that didn't work out. "Oh, I was so in love," Sara remembers. "His name was Avery Torgow, and he just left for California, and that was the end of it."

More than 50 years later, some of her friends remembered Avery as a nice looking guy with light hair, who went to California and later became a doctor. If he didn't love Sara, they said, he wasn't all that smart, nor was he worth worrying about. It was good riddance to Avery.

But, of course, that's not the way that Sara felt at the time. She was devastated. And the convergence of these two episodes—the love affair echoing her grief over Leonard—came as close to defeating Sara's spirit as anything in her life. She became extremely depressed and despondent. "It had quite an effect on me," she remembers. "I just couldn't get out of bed."

During college, Sara had become quite run down, sick and anemic. She had gone to visit her sister Helen, who was living in Chicago and, at that time, had met a neighbor who helped her enormously. "Mrs. Lazarre, a lovely woman, invited me up to lunch and shared her thoughts on Christian Science with me," Sara says. "There was a Christian Science church right across the street from where Helen lived. And so I started to attend the services there and became very attracted to its philosophy. I think it helped me get better. And when I got back to Detroit, I pursued it, and the more I pursued it, the more I became involved with it and the more interested in it I was."

After Leonard's disappearance and Avery Torgow's departure, Sara simply could not regain her energy. For a while she just couldn't move. But then she remembered her previous healing and she began to study Christian Science in earnest. She knew she was sick at heart and sick inside of herself. She desperately wanted to understand and overcome her deep sadness. With the counseling and work she did with a Christian Science practitioner named Marion Reading, Sara eventually overcame the paralysis of grief that had enfolded her. She also gained new understanding from reading *Science and Health* by Mary Baker Eddy, the founder of Christian Science. "I would say that I did have a healing," Sara says. "And it was that experience that gave me some peace about Leonard and brought me to Science."

In Christian Science, Sara found a system of religious teaching, based on scriptures, that applied mental and spiritual means to the treatment of disease—a scientific system of divine healing. As Mary Baker Eddy wrote in 1866, "A change in human belief changes all the physical symptoms, and determines a case for better or worse. When one's false belief is corrected, Truth sends a report of health all over the body."

Sara didn't talk with her family about her change of view and her deepening sense of self, her deepening sense of peace. But the change showed. "We just knew," her niece Philly remembers. "We would see her with this book all the time. She never just said it; she was always with the book. But look, don't knock it. Now in medical schools, they're teaching that your positive thinking has a lot to do with the healing of different diseases."

Sara had found a philosophy and a way of life that spoke to her of the laws of goodness and of universal harmony. The philosophy spoke to the kind of optimism that came to her naturally, the kind of optimism she had inherited from her mother. The religious tenets of Christian Science reinforced her belief that much of what we do and feel is controlled by our mental attitude. A negative attitude, she learned, achieves negative results and, likewise, *right thinking* or a positive attitude allows for a positive outcome. This philosophy clarified and defined an attitude and an approach she would put into practice for the rest of her life.

"I believe there is no such thing as a coincidence," says Sara. *"There is one plan for each of us, and when we listen and obey these angel thoughts, God will give us the right answer to every problem."*

Chapter 5

A NICE JEWISH BOY STEPS
ON STAGE

AFTER SARA'S SECOND YEAR AT B'nai Moshe Sunday School, "a nice Jewish boy," just the kind her parents had hoped and prayed for, came onto the scene. This happened when Ben Chinitz took over Irwin Shaw's job as principal of the Sunday school. One of Ben's closest friends was Melvyn Maxwell Smith, known at the time to various people as Max, Maxwell, Maxy and Melvyn. Eventually Sara would dub him "Smithy," but that didn't happen for quite some time. Ben and Max had grown up together on Alger Street, and when Ben learned that the Sunday school staff wanted to put out a publication, he thought Max, who had become a high school literature teacher, would be perfect for the job.

And so it was that at the first faculty meeting called by Ben Chinitz, Sara stepped into the room and saw a new face—one that was lean and chiseled, with curly brown hair, lively brown eyes and a quick smile. "Something about Maxwell Smith appealed to me right away," Sara remembers. "There was just something about him. It was the look in his eyes, the smile on his face, and his whole attitude, it was very very attractive to me. Before the meeting started, Ben asked if someone would volunteer to go across the street and purchase some refreshments. I said I would go, Maxwell said he would go, and another couple also volunteered. So the four of us dashed across the street to the drugstore, and we purchased all kinds of goodies and sweet things. We were having a lot of camaraderie and fun. We all came back to the meeting and my heart was thumping. I had just never met anyone who got that kind of reaction from me."

After a few weeks, Maxwell began taking Sara and a couple of other teachers for rides home in his car after Sunday school. Sara noticed that although he didn't ask her out for a date or express any real interest, he always dropped the others off first and took her home last. As a result, Sara began to learn a lot of things about Melvyn Maxwell Smith.

Like most of his friends on Alger Street, Smithy was the child of immigrants. Like Sara's parents, his parents, Isaac and Fannie Smith, had been born in Lithuania. Of course *Smith* was not Isaac's name before he arrived in America. Isaac's name, and the name of his father and grandfather and great-grandfather before him, was *Smiefsky*. But the name Smiefsky had gotten lost at the immigration table when a clerk asked Isaac his occupation. When Isaac answered that he was a carriage and harness maker, as well as a blacksmith who dealt with saddle horses, the immigration clerk is said to have proclaimed, "Ah, a smithy! Smith it shall be!"

Isaac and Fannie, like the Steins, kept a devout kosher home and went to synagogue often, thanking God for their blessings, which included five boys and three girls—Lou, Jack, Al, Maxwell, Marty, Jennie, Betty and Lillian. In 1920, the whole family moved from an apartment to their own home at 622 Alger Street. By that time, Jacob had his own carriage and harness shop, and over time, he bought several buildings on Hastings Avenue and rented out space to shopkeepers.

A favorite family story recalls a day when Henry Ford sent his financial representative into Isaac Smith's carriage and harness shop and offered to buy Isaac's business in exchange for stock in his new motor car company, which was beginning to build Model-T's. Ford's representative proposed that Isaac not only sell his shop, but also asked if he would be willing to help them make Model-T bodies for the Ford Motor Company.

"It makes no sense for me to sell my business to Ford Motor Company," Isaac is said to have responded. "Why should I sell my business to a buyer who wants to put me out of business?" Of course, today, family members telling the story say they wish Isaac could have seen into the future and changed his answer.

But Isaac Smith didn't live long enough to see how this new technology would permanently transform his business or transportation in America. His death, a couple of years after the family had moved to Alger Street, was recalled by Thomas J. Fraser, a childhood friend of Max and Marty's, in his memoirs, *One Block on Alger*, which was dedicated to Melvyn Maxwell Smith. "The funeral director had a big gray bus, and all of the family and mourners got in the bus with the casket sitting in the middle of it," he remembers. "We all proceeded to the cemetery for his burial."

Fraser also remembered Fannie Smith as a young widow raising her large family alone, making her regular trips by streetcar back to Hastings Avenue to collect the rents from the stores. "She used to spend most of the afternoon in her kitchen baking and preparing supper," Fraser wrote. "It seems that she always had a pot of borscht on the stove for any of the kids who were home for lunch."

In those Depression days in the late 1920s, movies were few and far between and television was non-existent, so the boys created their own fun. Kids of all ages, including Smithy, his younger brother Marty, Irv Rosen, Ben Chinitz, Harold Weiss, Milt Aptekar, and others, went to Moore Elementary School together, played baseball in the alley behind Alger Street or football in the empty lot nearby. They hung out at each other's houses, went to the library, and strolled over to Pulvers' Drug Store on the corner of Alger and Oakland to look at school supplies. Each year, these sons of immigrants would stand outside Pulver's window display of school supplies and figure out what they would be able to buy for 50 cents or a dollar—their total allotment for supplies. One year, Mr. Pulvers, the druggist, hired a man to stand absolutely still in the shop window. The man didn't move an eyelash for minutes at a time, and when he did, he moved as if he were a wooden soldier. This, of course, was a big event for the boys. Mr. Pulvers also used to give 50 cents worth of candy with every ten dollars of cash register receipts turned in, which encouraged the boys to hang around the front of the store waiting for customers to drop their receipts.

Pitching pennies was another favorite pastime. After the Jewish holidays in particular, when the adults had handed out lots of coins, the boys would hold pitching contests that ended with the closest penny taking them all. They also pitched in a bigger arena when they played baseball. Their baseball team, "The Swamp Angels," played in a vacant lot, where Maxwell and Marty headed every afternoon after leaving Hebrew school at a rabbi's house on King Avenue.

Even as a youngster, Smithy had a knack for attracting a wide variety of friends. Besides the instant crowd of his four brothers and two sisters, old and new friends also jammed onto his front porch in the summers and into his living room in the winters. "Max always seemed to have kids over," Fraser recalled. "We would spend hours on his front porch talking and joking around."

As a teenager at Northern High School in Detroit, Smithy had several friends who were musicians, including Milt Aptekar, a trumpeter who played in a jazz ensemble. (Aptekar later became a music teacher and formed a popular five-man orchestra that still plays at many events in the Detroit area.) Northern High, one of two very good high schools in Detroit, regularly competed with Central High, and school spirit was high. Smithy himself had a variety of talents and enthusiasms that contributed to the school and made him stand out. For one, he ran on Northern High's varsity track team, which gave him the privilege of being a varsity jock, wearing Northern's varsity letter on his sweater. Girls who liked the "lettered" boys particularly liked Smithy because he was friendly, polite, and a good dancer. Besides being a track star and academically very bright, Smithy also was captain of Northern's all-male cheerleading squad—the one with the megaphone who led the cheers at all the football, basketball and baseball games, he was the one stirring the spirit, encouraging, rousing the crowds.

Tom Fraser remembers the serious dialogues the Alger Street boys had at the Smiths while they sat around on cane furniture topped with blue cushions. Tom belonged to the Woodward Avenue Presbyterian Church boy scout troop, while Smithy was with a troop based at Temple Beth El. "I never got to be more than a tenderfoot," Fraser says, "but Maxie went all the way to become an Eagle Scout with many merit badges."

Through scouting, Smithy found a place to belong, to build skills along with confidence. He also experienced trekking and camping, tree and plant identification, fishing and other outdoor skills. Later he would say that scouting had triggered his love affair with nature, taught him the discipline that allowed him to work towards goals he believed he could accomplish, and turned him into a devoted conservationist. Outdoors, close to trees and along the streams, Smithy always found great peace of mind and a communion with God. He liked to quote Emily Dickinson, saying that her words reflected his own feeling. Often he would quote her:

> *Some keep the Sabbath going to church.*
> *I keep it staying at home,*
> *with a bobbling forecaster*
> *and an orchard for a dome.*

In many ways, Smithy and his friends were preparing for the future—for their lives, their careers, their families. Tom Fraser remembers that Marty, even as a boy, wanted to be a dentist. "Marty claimed there was not enough money in teaching, but Max and I both agreed we would be satisfied with $35 per week—the going rate for teachers at that time—for the rest of our lives," Tom Fraser recalled.

During those years, the question of how to make a living was critical. The boys on Alger Street, like many others, had the ambition to get out of school and do something positive with their lives—something practical and stable enough to put and keep food on the table. "The catchword in those days was security," says Harold Weiss, who was in the same grade room, Thomas Edison House—House #208, at Northern High as Smithy. "Security was civil service or teaching or social work, which also was secure, because people would always need social work. They were poor! We were the children of immigrants who, in this new land, wanted to be more than our parents. They pushed us to get an education. To be good people. Study and work hard. They wanted us to be good citizens, and as a corollary to the hard work and study, they wanted us to save our money. We were products of that environment."

The family's focus on security, as well as a lack of funds and the realities of the Depression put a quash on Melvyn Maxwell Smith's dreams of studying architecture when he went to college. In 1932, he applied to the University of Michigan's architectural school and was accepted. But, because his brother Marty needed to go to the University of Michigan to become a dentist, the Smith family decided that they couldn't afford to send both boys to Ann Arbor. They suggested that Maxwell go to the cheaper and next best option—the City College of Detroit, which later would become Wayne State University—for at least two years. Then, perhaps, they could send him to Michigan to complete his degree in architecture.

At the time, tuition at City College was $56 a semester and the entire school was located in one building. During his first semester there, Maxwell was deeply affected by an English professor named Miss Boyer. This professor introduced him to Emerson and Thoreau and the concepts of transcendentalism. Smithy came to believe that people obtained their knowledge of reality from intuitive sources rather than objective experiences. The discussions not only excited his imagination and broadened the way he looked at the world, but they gave him a transcendent feeling about life and about himself. He decided that if teaching could so radically affect a student's life—as Miss Boyer had affected his—he wanted to become a teacher, too. He wanted to be that useful, that creative, that valuable. What could be more satisfying? At that point in time, Maxwell decided that he wouldn't go to Ann Arbor to be an architect, even if the opportunity presented itself. He wanted to stay at City College and become a teacher.

After he graduated with a bachelor's degree in education and in literature, Smithy, like his friends, began looking for a job. Jobs in general weren't easy to come by, and getting a teaching job in Detroit was particularly difficult. Initially, he got a job as a grade school teacher at the Bishop School. But eventually, he would receive a promotion and become a high school English teacher, and for the rest of his career, he would teach literature to teenagers, serve as sponsor for the yearbook, and "coach" dancing classes after school. Smithy had a passion for teaching, and believed that literature was a wonderful way to open the students' eyes to life and to get them to understand what makes people do what they do. He often said it was a privilege to be able to teach literature and to read and hear poetry read aloud. Students often recalled being mesmerized by his interpretive readings.

After his first year of teaching, Smithy set out to get his doctorate at what by then had become Wayne State University. It was there, during his graduate classes, that he had an experience that was to shape the rest of his life. This defining experience happened in an art history and humanities class taught by Dr. Betsy Jane Welling, who was known as a remarkable professor. "One of the visual art media forms that we studied was architecture," Smithy recalled during an interview with architectural writer A. Dale Northup in 1979. "It was during the last 15 to 20 minutes of the entire semester, when we arrived at a brief study of contemporary architecture, that I saw a projection of Frank Lloyd Wright's "Fallingwater" house in Bear Run, Pennsylvania, on the screen. I exclaimed to the instructor, 'Who did that?!'

"And she said, 'Frank Lloyd Wright.'"

Others in the class remember that moment well. It was something so out of the ordinary, so bizarre on some level, so serendipitous, so seemingly comic. With the drama of this phenomenal house suspended over a waterfall on the projected screen in front of them, Smithy leaped out of his seat and, with extraordinary excitement and passion in his voice, he yelled, "Someday I'm going to own a Frank Lloyd Wright house!"

After a moment of shock, the entire class started laughing. They roared with laughter. Frank Lloyd Wright was a world-renowned architect. He was famous, brilliant, a master! And Smithy was a regular Joe, just like them! They had just learned that Wright had designed the Ravine Bluffs Bridge in Illinois; the Imperial Hotel in Tokyo; the "Hollyhock House" on Olive Hill in Los Angeles; a famous house for Tazaemon Yamamura in Japan; and the Freeman House and the Charles Ennis House in Los Angeles. And at the time, he was close to completing the extraordinary Johnson Wax Company's administration building in Racine, Wisconsin. Dealing with this architect meant big money; he didn't design homes in exchange for peanuts.

One of his classmates—and Sara's old camp partner—remembers the moment well. "I was there when he stood up and yelled, 'I'm going to own a Frank Lloyd Wright house,' Irv Rosen recalls. "I said, 'Smithy, how can you say you're going to own a house by him? He's a world-renowned architect! And on your teacher's salary of seven dollars a day, how are you going to make it?'

"'I'm going to make it,' he says. 'I'm going to make it. That's going to be one of the things I'm going to do.'

"I said, 'More power to you!' But I never believed it. That was my big mistake. I never believed he could do it!"

But after seeing that slide of Fallingwater, life for Smithy was never the same.

After class, he went directly to the Detroit main library and looked up every article he could find on Frank Lloyd Wright. "I discovered that Wright not only was able to draw well, but he wrote quite well about his phase of organic architecture," Smithy said. "There were a lot of articles in the clip files, and I spent about ten days both in and outside of the library becoming a bibliophile on the architect's work. I read everything available at the time.

"It was in one of the magazines, *Architectural Forum* of January 1938, that had published Wright's more recent works, that I discovered that Wright not only designed large buildings and residences for wealthy clients, but also had undertaken a residence for a client of moderate means. A budding young journalist out of Madison, Wisconsin, Herbert Jacobs, had challenged Mr. Wright with the remark, 'Could you build me a house for $5,000?' and Mr. Wright had responded by telling Mr. Jacobs he would certainly try. When I read that, I realized that *I*, too, could afford a house by Frank Lloyd Wright."

Smithy determined there and then that this passion he had for Frank Lloyd Wright's work and philosophy would never be just a passing fancy. He eventually *would* live in a house designed personally by Frank Lloyd Wright. He didn't know how it would happen, but it *would* happen. And any woman he married would have to be willing to live there with him. Otherwise, she wouldn't be the right woman for him.

TOP: Thelma, Sara and Leonard Stein in Johnstown, Pa. LEFT: Leonard at age 3. RIGHT: Sara, 20, in 1927 audition photo.

TOP: Sara, Assistant Director of Girls, and fellow counselors at Fresh Air Camp in 1938. LEFT: Sara with Camp Director Irwin Shaw. RIGHT: Sara with Assistant Director of Boys Irving Rosen.

Sara as a student at Michigan Normal.

ABOVE: Smithy and Sara on their honeymoon in the Smokey Mountains of Tennessee in 1940.

OPPOSITE, TOP: Melvyn Maxwell Smith is inducted into the Armed Forces in 1941. RIGHT: Smithy and Sara together in Atlantic City during World War II.

CLOCKWISE FROM TOP LEFT: Sara with Bobby in 1944; Smithy and Bobby; Sara and Bobby; Bobby in 1946.

TOP: Bobby, age 5, showing his Aunt Helen and Uncle Al Ross and other family and friends the newly purchased property in Bloomfield Hills, Michigan. LEFT: Sara and Smithy resume teaching in the Detroit public school system. RIGHT: Smithy's yearbook picture for the *Cody Comet* in the mid-1950s.

Sara with her sisters (*from left*) Minnie, Thelma and Helen in the early 1950s.

ABOVE: Sara working as a counselor at the Cranbrook Summer Theater School in the 1960s. BELOW: Sara directing students in a Cranbrook Summer Theater School musical.

Sara and Smithy with Bob and Anne at their wedding in 1971.

Sara and Smithy at their home in the late 1970s.

ABOVE, LEFT: Sara with her grandchildren Michael and Jennifer in 1978. ABOVE, RIGHT: Sara and Smithy at an art opening. BELOW: Sara, acting in "A Flea in Her Ear," takes a break with her fellow cast members in the St. Dunston's Theater production.

Sara and Smithy receiving the Anthony Wayne Society Award for outstanding
service to Wayne State University.

ABOVE: On the terrace of *My Haven*: The last Smith family picture, taken shortly before Smithy's death in July, 1984.

OPPOSITE: Sara in Santa Barbara with Bob, Michael, Anne and Jennifer in 1998.

Sara Smith in Santa Barbara, 1998.

"In order to find happiness in your surroundings," says Sara,
"you first have to find happiness in yourself"

Chapter 6

THE BUMPY ROAD
TO LOVE

Later, sara would say, "I fell in love with this man immediately, but it took him almost three years to realize that I was the one he wanted to marry."

At the time, Sara, Smithy and most of the other B'nai Moshe Sunday school teachers, including Irv Rosen, Sara Horowitz and Ben Chinitz, were also teachers in the Detroit public school system. At Sunday school, they not only did volunteer teaching, but they all had their specialties. Sara's specialty was working on dramatic presentations with the children, and Smithy's was putting out a weekly newspaper with the help of the students.

Smithy had high standards; he expected excellence and he got it. "It's not easy to make 15- and 16-year olds give up an evening and say yes, we'll come extra nights to the synagogue so we can publish a newspaper," says Ben Chinitz, who watched Smithy's skill with the students. "But Smithy had a bond with them, and each week, they would put out a newspaper for the other students. These were the days before copy machines; you had to cut the stencils and crank out the newsletters. And this was all extra time for the teachers. None of us got paid anything for it. We must have had 300 or 400 students. We volunteered at least 15 hours a week at the Sunday school, and that was on top of our regular teaching."

Sara's students would come to the synagogue during the week and at nights to rehearse for plays and dramatic presentations, which they often performed during Sunday school hours. They loved working with

Sara, who made them feel good about themselves, made them understand that they could do anything on the stage and then carry that confidence with them when they returned home.

"Both of them were mesmerizers in their respective fields," Ben Chinitz recalls. "They both did outstanding things. Sunday school for adolescents is not easy, but both Sara and Smithy had the students coming in extra. They were both that devoted to their work."

And through the work and the contact, a friendship was developing. For Sara, however, it was more than friendship. "The more I saw Maxwell, the more I was attracted to him," she says. "I wanted to see him more than just on Sundays, so I started having parties and picnics and all kinds of get-togethers at my home, and I would invite the Sunday school faculty. Maxwell always came to the parties, but he never asked me for a date."

Years later, Ben Chinitz recalled the frequent gatherings at the Stein home. "When you walked into the Stein home, you were just taken over by the warmth, the complete warmth," he says. "We played cards, we drank tea, and we would sing! Everybody would sing, everybody would have fun. People went there because they wanted to have closeness and have a good time. Sara's sisters had the same warmth, the same enthusiasm for people that Sara had. They had the same friendliness, the same concern. This home was always open to everyone. The lights were always on, and you could stop by any time of day or night."

Sara's first "date" with Smithy was not by invitation. It happened one night when a friend of Sara's named Melba Sklar asked Sara if she would do the makeup for the actors in a small play she was directing at B'nai Moshe. Sara agreed, and took Sara Horowitz, her friend and former college roommate, along. Maxwell and Ben were at the performance, and afterwards, they asked if they could drive the girls home. Ben drove, and Sara Horowitz sat in the front with him. Sara sat in the back seat with Smithy. "As we were driving, Maxwell put his arm around me and started to kiss me," Sara remembers. "I pushed him away. I really wanted to kiss him, but I thought that would be necking, and a kiss was a very sacred thing to me. Also, I didn't want to kiss him with another couple up in the front seat. When I pushed him away, he got very angry, and when we got out in front of my home, he opened the door of the car and let me out. Then he got right back into the car and slammed the door. He was so insulted that I wouldn't kiss him. I walked up the walk, up my front stairs and went into the house. But we still remained friends, and he still drove me home on Sundays with the other girls."

When June arrived, it also signaled the closing of the temple's Sunday school for summer vacation. Just the thought of not seeing Maxwell until September made Sara sad, so she decided to arrange several summer picnics for the Sunday school faculty. At one of the first of those picnics, she introduced a girlfriend of hers to Maxwell, and Maxwell fell hard for the girl. "I introduced them," says Sara. "But I always believed that no one else could have whoever was planned for me. Maxwell fell in love with her, and later, she told me he wanted to marry her. But she was already pledged to a young man in Chicago, and she said that she told him he should date Sara Stein." Quick to ruffle, Smithy told the girl basically to mind her own business; he would date whom he pleased.

Rozanne, the secretary of the Sunday school, was the one who arranged Sara's first "official" date with Smithy in the spring of 1939. Rozanne belonged to a club that always had a special party at the end of their season. That year they had extra money and decided to invite another couple to join their group at a special place outside Detroit called The Hungarian Village. The secretary decided to invite Max Smith and Sara Stein, and she arranged for Max to pick Sara up at home and drive her to the party. "I was so excited, happy and thrilled to be his date," Sara remembers. "I did everything to make myself presentable. I wasn't too much on clothes, and I certainly didn't look like anything that stepped out of Vogue. But I never lacked for conversation. Maxwell called for me, and we drove down to the Hungarian Village, which was over an hour's drive away. We talked and laughed and had fun, and I was in ecstasy. He was very courteous and, of course, he was dressed to perfection.

"At the Hungarian village we were seated at a table for eight. Maxwell danced exactly one dance with me, which was the polite thing to do. After he danced with me, I enjoyed watching him dance with the other girls. He was a beautiful dancer—he taught dancing at the high school—and it was a delight to just sit there and watch him dance. I did not feel jealous or left out. I just had a feeling of admiration.

"I'll admit that as I watched him, passion was aroused within me. When it was time to go home, Rozanne asked Maxwell if he would drive her and her date home. They had come with another couple and didn't have their own car. Somehow or other, I felt it was all contrived on her part, because I thought she liked Maxwell, too. But when we all got into the car, I felt such a great desire to kiss this boy that I said to myself, 'If Maxwell takes Rozanne and her date home first, I will make an attempt to kiss him.' Well, as it happened, he took Rozanne's date home first, and then he drove to Rozanne's, walked her up to her door and then got back into the car. As soon as he got back into the car and started to drive, I put my arms around him, ready to kiss him, and he said, 'Can't you wait until we park?' Rozanne lived only a short distance from my home. So I waited until we parked in front of my home.

"No sooner did we park than we put our arms around one another and I gave him a real soul kiss. Even I was surprised at the kiss I gave him. It was just a kiss, and no other part of the body was touched, but it was beautiful. Then we kissed again and again. Then we left the car, and he took me up to the door. When he said goodnight, he gave me the sweetest kiss on my lips.

"I walked into the house and everyone was sleeping. I decided to get ready for bed, and I walked into the bathroom and looked into the mirror at a very red-faced girl, and said, "I am engaged!" How naive can you be. But that's the way I felt; I really thought I was engaged. That is what this kiss meant to me.

"Well, that was Saturday night, and the next morning I got up and went to Sunday school and started to teach my class. I was on Cloud 9. I could hardly wait to see Maxwell, and I knew I would see him at the faculty meeting we always had at the end of the morning session."

When Sara walked into the meeting room, however, she overheard Smithy talking to Saul Schlesinger, the young man she had worked with in the children's theater. They didn't see her, and before she had a chance to say anything, she heard Maxwell talking to Saul in a confidential way. Maxwell was saying, "Oh was she a date! Still water certainly runs deep! What a wonderful date she was!"

"I couldn't believe what I was hearing, but I heard it," Sara says. "Well, I sat down on the chair and just wished that the floor would open up and swallow me. I was devastated to think that he didn't take those kisses seriously. After the meeting I ran out of the room and called my mother and told her I needed a ride home. My feelings were turned totally against Melvyn Maxwell Smith. I didn't want to be in his company, and I didn't ride home with him from Sunday school that day or any day following!

"Of course, I knew after what I'd heard that I would get a call from Saul Schlesinger, and it happened. No sooner did I get home from Sunday school than the phone rang, and there was Saul—who I'd worked with and known for two years and never dated!—and he was asking me for a date for the next evening. Saul, of course, was going to find out how *deep* those still waters were. I gave him a date, and I believe we went to the theater and got a bite to eat. Then we came home, and Saul started taking off his coat and loosening his tie for action. I knew what he had in mind. I said, 'I'm very tired, and I want to get to bed as early as I can.' I helped him on with his jacket, handed him his tie and sent him on his way, figuring he probably was wondering what Maxwell was talking about?"

Sara, who never wanted to see Melvyn Maxwell Smith again, made a point of ignoring him. "At Sunday school, I would never bid Maxwell the time of day," she says. "I would never look at him or talk to him. All my love that I had for him turned into repulsion. It's strange, but that's what happened.

"I was a good rebound for someone, and the person I fell in love with was Albert Corlinko, who was a driver for my father. My father was still a manufacturer's representative, and at the time, he was representing Zero King Jackets. He didn't drive. Also, the sample cases were very heavy, and so my father always had someone drive his car and carry the sample cases into the store. He'd had many drivers work for him, but at the time he had Albert, a delightful and charming young man from New

York. The whole family fell in love with Albert, and he and I were very good friends. Albert was Jewish, and he was a very personable young man. When he wasn't with Dad, Albert was always around the house and would take the family anywhere they wanted to go. So Albert started taking me to Sunday school on Sunday mornings, and then at 12 o'clock, he would be at the synagogue to pick me up and take me home. Albert was so available, so kind, that my affections went out to him. We would go for long rides, and of course, we kissed. He was so dear and so kind, so patient and so loving, that I really fell in love with him, and I decided that I wanted to marry him.

"Albert said he wasn't good enough for me. One time he said, 'You ought to marry someone like Smithy.' I told him I wasn't interested in Smithy anymore, but I was interested in him." Albert was just a high school graduate, but he was a good dancer, and Sara had the idea that she could set him up in a dancing school, and that a marriage between them could work out.

At first Sara's family didn't know that she was dating Albert. The fact that the two went for long rides didn't raise suspicions. But when Sara's father found out what was going on, he wasn't happy. "When my father found out that I was in love with Albert, he practically had a heart attack," Sara says. She doesn't make any connection between her father's horror and the fact that in June, Albert decided that he was going to leave her father's employment and head down South. "I was devastated because I had really learned to love this boy," Sara says. "We had plans that we would write and keep in touch, and we even thought we would elope during Christmas vacation. But you know, I never heard from Albert again."

About a week after Albert left, Smithy called Sara and told her that his sister Jennie was giving a graduation party for his brother and himself, and he would like her to be his date for the evening. He said Marty was receiving his degree in dentistry from the University of Michigan, while Maxwell was receiving his master's degree in literature. "I still had that horrible feeling toward him," Sara says, "and I told him I was invited to a wedding that day, and my answer was no. Even if I hadn't been busy, I would not have gone with him anyway."

After the June graduation from Sunday school, Smithy came up to Sara and told her that he would be gone for the summer. He was driving his family out to California and then up to British Columbia, but he had a favor to ask of Sara. His niece, Barbara, was going to be a camper at the Fresh Air camp, and he wondered if Sara would give her a little attention and see that she was well taken care of. "I'd appreciate it if you would look in on her once in a while," he said. Sara, who was still very angry at Maxwell, coldly replied, "I will try."

During that summer at Fresh Air camp, Sara and Irv Rosen worked together again and had a great summer. She loved the work of planning schedules, meals and entertainment that went hand in hand with swimming, game playing, dramatic presentations, plays and parties with the children. During the summer, she got a number of cards from Smithy, but she wasn't happy to be receiving them. She would read them and then toss them right into the waste paper basket. She did look in on Barbara a few times, and was glad to see that Barbara was doing very well without any need for intervention on her part.

On the last day of camp, when parents were coming for their children, all of the staff dressed in white. Sara, barely five-feet tall, had lost a lot of weight over the summer and was wearing a pair of size four white shorts and a thin white blouse. She felt very slim and attractive that summer, and good about herself. She was talking to some children when suddenly, there in front of her was none other than Melvyn Maxwell Smith. "His eyes just seemed to eat me up," she says. "I could tell he was very impressed with me, and he tried to be very friendly. I didn't even offer my hand. I just said "Hi." He asked me about his niece, Barbara, and I said I thought she'd gotten along very well. Then I said I had many things that had to be taken care of, and off I went. I felt his eyes following me, but I had absolutely no good feeling whatsoever for him. I also managed not to see him during the rest of that day."

After camp was over, Sara went back to Detroit to prepare for her new post as an elementary school literature teacher at the Fairbanks School. But schools closed for two weeks because of a contagious disease, so Sara decided to go to Chicago to visit her sister Helen. Helen always had been a striking dresser and had a great sense of fashion. "I had all this money and I said to Helen, 'You know, I'm just going to spend all this money on clothes!'" So Helen took Sara on a shopping spree, and Sara purchased hats, gloves, purses, sportswear, dresses and gowns—and did, in fact, spend every bit of the money she had earned at camp.

When she got back to Detroit two days before school opened, she heard that Maxwell had received a promotion to Chadsey High School, and so she sent him a card congratulating him. He called to thank her, and during their conversation, she told him that she'd been transferred from kindergarten to elementary school literature. Smithy said that since he had just left elementary school literature, he would be happy to give her all of his teaching materials. "I knew that Maxwell was an outstanding teacher and probably would have a lot of material that would help me," Sara said. "I accepted the offer and he brought it right over. I was grateful, but I still had a resentful attitude towards him. My dad happened to be home when Maxwell arrived, and after Maxwell left, my dad said, 'Now Sara, that is a nice young man. I would like you to see more of him.'"

Sara made no comment. Her father was concerned about Sara's prospects for marrying because she was almost 30, and all of her sisters had married in their early twenties. He had brought a number of eligible and successful businessmen to the house, but Sara never seemed interested in his choices. "I remember one of them owned a chain of drug stores, and I was trapped into meeting him," Sara says. "He was wearing a powder blue suit, and just the color of the suit alone turned me off. After I met him, I made some excuse that I had an appointment and left. Another man was planning our honeymoon in Europe even before we had a friendship started. I got out of that one fast. My father was a little worried about me getting married, but I certainly wasn't worried."

Sara wasn't interested in marrying someone just to get married. Most particularly, she was not interested in seeing any more of Melvyn Maxwell Smith, and she had no intention of doing so to placate her father's anxieties. She had a strong sense of herself, and while she always seemed cooperative and polite to her father, she was in truth very stubborn about doing exactly what she wanted to do.

A few days later, Maxwell called and asked Sara to go with him to see *Gone With the Wind* on Saturday. Being a nice and well-mannered girl, she didn't just say no; she gave him an excuse for being unable to go.

"Oh, I'm sorry," she said. I can't go because I'm meeting Ben at the Sunday school to organize some materials for the year."

"Oh, that won't interfere at all," Maxwell said. "Ben and his date are going to be part of the group, too, so I'm sure your meeting won't be lasting that long."

"He said there were about five couples that would see *Gone With the Wind* together and then we'd go out afterwards for a bite to eat," Sara recalls. "I felt trapped then, so I said, 'Well, alright, I'll go.' He told me what time he would pick me up, and I said, 'Fine.'

"Well, that Saturday night, now that I had a closet full of beautiful clothes, I selected a lovely, casual black dress that had two rows of buttons all the way down the front. At that time, they were wearing those Clara Bow hats that had a big bow in front of the hat, and I wore that and gloves, with new shoes and jewelry to match—with everything coordinated perfectly. Every girl wants to look nice for a man—no matter who it is. I really looked like a beautiful little model, and when Maxwell came into the living room and looked at me and my beautiful outfit, you could tell he was overwhelmed and overjoyed.

"We started out, and conversation was very easy for me and for him, too, so we talked all the way downtown. When we were walking on Washington Boulevard that night, he was so happy that he even jumped over a fire hydrant. *Gone with the Wind* is a long show—about four hours—but it was great, and everybody seemed to enjoy it. Then afterwards, we all went to a road house out on North Woodward called the Northwood Inn. They had dancing there, and food, and we all sat at a table together talking and laughing. Pretty soon Maxwell asked me to dance, and while we were dancing, he started telling me his plans for what we were going to do in October and November. I was thinking, 'Boy, you are just lucky you have this date with me tonight.' I figured this would be his last date with me. I had vowed that if he tried to kiss me, I would *never* go out with him again. I still did not feel very warmly towards him, and that awful feeling of repulsion would just not go away.

"When we got to the house, he got out, walked around the car, opened the door for me and walked me up to the door. Then he took my hand, and he said, 'Goodnight. I hope to see you real soon.' I thanked him, said goodnight and walked into the house feeling very pleased that he didn't attempt to come in the house or try to make advances.

"A few days later, he called again and asked me out for another date. I believe it was to go to dinner and the theater on Friday night. I accepted, and of course, again, I had quite a choice of clothes to wear. I remember deciding I would wear this good-looking dress that had a velvet top and scotch plaid skirt, with a repetition of scotch plaid in the scarf. I guess inwardly I wanted to make an impression on Melvyn Maxwell Smith, even though I didn't feel lovingly towards him.

"During that week, Wayne University Workshop Theater held try-outs for *Our Town*, and the director, Mr. Dunham, asked me to try out for Mrs. Gibbs, the mother of George. I tried out for it and got that part, which rather thrilled me. I enjoyed the character and I loved working in pantomime with imaginary props.

"Well, when Friday night came and Maxwell arrived, the whole family was very happy to see him. We talked for a little while with the family before we left. On our way to dinner, I told him about getting the part of Mrs. Gibbs in *Our Town*. He seemed thrilled about it. He knew I was interested in theater, and he said, 'You know, I would love to pick you up after rehearsals and bring you home.' I usually got a ride with one of my fellow workers, but sometimes I had to take the bus home, and this sounded very convenient and very nice, and I accepted. Rehearsals were usually Sunday, Monday, Wednesday and Friday nights, and Maxwell didn't miss one rehearsal. This meant that we saw a great deal of one another that fall. But not once did we kiss. This was on a very friendly basis and a hand shake when he dropped me off and walked me to my door. Years later, he would always say how much he enjoyed being a Stage Door Johnny; he would stay and watch every rehearsal.

"The play ended just before my birthday, which was November 7th. And on my birthday, when I arrived home from school, there on the baby grand was a huge arrangement of beautiful flowers that literally covered the top of the piano. They were from Maxwell, and I was not one bit pleased. I didn't want a gift from him. Even though we were friendly, I still had a very negative feeling about anything even vaguely romantic with him."

Sara's father, who was home at the time, said, "Sara, you should call Maxwell and thank him for these beautiful flowers."

"I will when I feel like it," Sara said.

"Very reluctantly," Sara says, she did go to the phone and call Smithy, thanking him for the flowers. During the call, he asked her for another date that Saturday evening, and again, she accepted. That Saturday, he took her to one of the most elegant restaurants in Detroit, and she realized how proud he was to be with her. After that, they began to go out quite often, but always by themselves. No one at the Sunday school even knew they were going out.

"Eventually, that cold, awful feeling of hurt disappeared," says Sara, "and little by little, the love I felt for him when I first met him started to come back. He was so loving, and he expressed the most beautiful spiritual qualities. I couldn't help falling in love with him again. He wasn't at all demanding—just kind and considerate and fun. We had a great time going places and just enjoying one another's company so much. He would talk about what we were going to do in January and February and March, and he kept talking about all the wonderful things we would do in the future. He gave me an inkling that he wanted this to go on forever and forever."

As they became more spontaneous with each other, Sara admitted that she had never particularly liked the name Melvyn or Maxwell. One evening they went to a movie, and in it, the male lead was called Smithy. Sara asked Maxwell if he would mind if she called him Smithy, and he said he rather liked that name, too. "From then on, he became Smithy to me," Sara says, "And he also became Smithy to his family and to many of our friends."

During the month of December, Sara and Smithy began talking about the idea of marriage. Their discussions weren't so much about the matter of whether or not they should marry, but how, where and when. "Both of us were blissfully happy," says Sara. "On New Year's Eve, Smithy took me out for a late dinner at Frame's Restaurant, a beautiful place in downtown Detroit. The setting on the table was so exquisite, and he, of course, proposed.

"What a beautiful time we had. I will never forget that dinner. Afterwards, when we got into the car, Maxwell gave me my ring. This ring was one he had bought the year before from an artisan from India who had come to the synagogue. I had met this artisan and introduced him to the faculty, and he had showed the faculty all his beautiful hand-crafted jewelry. Smithy was very interested in it, and he gave the man a commission to make an engagement ring for the girl he was going to marry—even though he didn't know who he was going to marry! The engagement ring that he designed was the ring he gave me on that evening, December 31, 1939."

Sara and Smithy went to the Stein house to tell them about their engagement. Even though it was late, everyone was still up and visiting in the kitchen.

Before they got to the door of the kitchen, however, Maxwell said, "Maybe we shouldn't show the family the ring."

"Why not?"

"Oh, I don't know. It's not a diamond. It's so big, but it's just a moonstone."

"That's ridiculous! It's beautiful!"

"But it cost less than a hundred dollars."

"Of course I'm going to show it to them! I'm not interested in diamonds or rubies or emeralds. I'm interested in the beautiful man I'm going to marry."

Sara called her family in, and one by one they all came into the living room. She showed them her hand with the ring on it, and everyone was kissing and hugging and yelling *Mazel Tov! Mazel Tov!* "Of course, Maxwell had already asked my father's permission to marry me, and my father had said, 'By all means, my son!'" Sara remembers. "Oh what happiness filled the atmosphere. My dad said, 'Well, we should call up Smithy's mother and see if she would like to come over.' So he called her up, and we all talked to her, but she said she wouldn't be able to come over because she was leaving for Florida the next day and it would be just too much for her. Well, we tried to understand, and we continued to celebrate. We called up Helen in Chicago and Essie in Indian-apolis, and they were so delighted! It was such a wonderful night.

"From that time on, Smithy and I were together every evening, and there were many nights we didn't get home until one or two in the morning. Of course that wasn't so great because we had to get up very early for school. But our happiness kept us going.

"When we returned to Sunday school after vacation and the teach-ers saw the ring on my engagement finger, they were floored because no one knew we'd been going out. But they were excited and happy. There were showers and all kinds of parties."

Two people who weren't particularly happy about Smithy and Sara at the beginning were Sara Horowitz and little cousin, 14-year-old Phyllis. Sara Horowitz felt betrayed because Sara hadn't confided in her, and Philly was jealous that Sara didn't—and wouldn't—have as much time for her as she'd once had. "When he proposed, and when she was going to get married, I was really upset," Phyllis Clinton recalls. "I really didn't like him, and I said to her, 'It'll never be the same between us. I was like a child whose mother is remarrying, and the child is jeal-ous!'" Eventually, however, both Sari and Phyllis found Sara's delight contagious. Both girls were pulled into the fun and excitement of help-ing Sara plan her wedding.

One of the plans that Sara and Smithy made concerned the way they would handle their religious beliefs with their families. Sara, of course, had told Smithy about her beliefs as a Christian Scientist. Although she was born into the Jewish faith, she said, she would never practice that faith in the same way her parents did, nor did she want to. She did not want to keep a kosher house or follow kosher dietary laws. Smithy confessed that he didn't really practice the orthodox Judaism of his parents either, because he was attracted to transcendentalism, the religion of Emerson, Thoreau and Kahlil Gibran. Maxwell told Sara that he had not announced his beliefs to his mother, and while it was fine with him for Sara not to practice Judaism, he would prefer that she didn't tell his mother or his family about it. If they knew, it would be too upsetting to them, and it just wasn't worth it. Sara promised she wouldn't tell his family, and she never did.

Another deep understanding between them involved Maxwell's dream to someday own a Frank Lloyd Wright house—the dream that had started when he first saw the slide of the "Fallingwater" home designed by the great architect. "Smithy always said that he would never marry anyone who wasn't willing to live in a Frank Lloyd Wright home," says Sara. "But I would have married Smithy even if we had to live in a tent!"

"The more we give," says Sara, *"the more we have to give."*

Chapter 7

LOVE AND MARRIAGE

SARA AND SMITHY were supposed to be married in June, but Sara had promised Irwin Shaw to return to the Fresh Air camp as assistant director again that summer, and she wasn't willing to go back on that commitment. Smithy thought that getting married in June and having his brand new wife rush off to camp would make him feel too lonely and terrible. "If we get married during Easter vacation, then I won't mind so much if you have to go off to camp for two months," Smithy told her. Sara agreed, and so they decided to move up their date. They would get married in March, during spring vacation.

They set the date for March 21st, which would allow them time for a honeymoon the following week. Helen and Thelma both had "hotel weddings," and Essie had eloped. But Sara wanted an at-home wedding, like Min's had been. It would be small, just her family and his, and each of them would invite one friend. Smithy had invited Ben Chinitz and Sara invited Sarah Horowitz. As for her bridal outfit, Sara didn't want to wear the typical white gown. Instead, she wanted the color to be a beautiful shade of blue. Sara's friend Richard Lapin, a singer and actor studying dress design in Chicago, told her that he wanted to design and make her wedding dress, and she was thrilled.

Sara and Richard had been friends for many years. She'd met him when he was a teenager, and Richard remembers how Sara got him involved in the theater, which became his life's work. ("I'm quite an introspective person," Richard said recently on a break from the Metropolitan Opera in New York City, where he still performs on stage at the age of 80. "Sara saw that immediately. But she has such a fey, childlike quality and she just pulled me in. I probably would have gotten there on my own anyway, but she made it happen much more quickly.")

Sara had seen Richard's costume designs for the Wayne State University Theater group, and she had also seen the wedding gown he had designed for his sister. She thought that a design by Richard Lapin was equal to any by Bill Blass. The only criterion she gave Richard was that he use the color blue. Otherwise, she left all the decisions to him. "I knew whatever he designed for me would make both Smithy and me very proud," she said. "We just took it for granted that the dress would be beautiful and that Richard would have it ready for the wedding by March 21st."

Two weeks before the wedding, however, the gown had not arrived. Sara didn't feel she could call Richard to ask when he was bringing the dress, so she and Smithy decided they would go shopping for an alternative—just in case Richard's dress didn't make it. "We knew the old tale that the groom isn't supposed to see your outfit before the wedding, but we did go shopping and picked out a beautiful blue dress with a matching coat," Sara says. "We were both very pleased with the way it looked."

The night before their wedding, Smithy was at Sara's house until about ten p.m., and then he went home. In the kitchen, Sara's sisters and her nieces were cooking food for the wedding reception, and the house was humming with activity. Thelma, a wonderful baker and cook, was directing the show. "We were making all these rolled up sandwiches," Phyllis Clinton remembers, "and my grandfather was so worried there wouldn't be enough food! So everybody was laughing. Aunt Rose was there telling her jokes, and we told Grandpa, 'Don't worry! If anybody takes more than three sandwiches, we'll slap their hands, that's all! We were up all night making those sandwiches and covering them with damp towels."

Soon after Smithy's departure, the doorbell rang. Sara opened it, and there was Richard Lapin with the wedding gown in his arms.

"Richard!" Sara said as she hugged and kissed him. "I had no idea you were going to bring the dress the day before the wedding."

"I promised you!" Richard said.

"I didn't think you were going to bring it at all," Sara laughed.

"But it's your wedding dress! How could I not bring it on time?!"

Sara jumped up and down with excitement. "It was a gorgeous, handmade, with frills of beautiful laces on the collar and down the center," she says. "And the bottom of the dress was all hand pleated. Of course Smithy didn't know anything about it, and we weren't about to tell him."

The next day, on her wedding day, which happened to be cold and snowy, Sara went to school to teach in the morning. "Imagine teaching on your wedding day!" she says. "At noon, Dad sent the car for me to go to a millinery shop not far from my home. I gave the woman some extra material Richard had given me for a turban, and she created a beautiful one for me. I was thrilled! When I got home, everybody loved the turban, and we were all excited as we got dressed."

"Sara was late for her own wedding!" Phyllis Clinton remembers. "She never had any conception of time, and she was late. Not just fifteen minutes late, but more like an hour. She ran in late and got dressed. I remember I was aggravated about it."

Sara recalls that the rabbi who was supposed to marry them got sick, so Ben Chinitz had to go and find another one for the ceremony. And Ben remembers another detail. "Of course, the orthodox rabbi requires that the bride have a veil covering her face," Ben says. "And when Rabbi Fischer finally joined us, he saw that Sara had no veil. So what do you do? You can't just proceed. I got in the car and started going down Linwood and Dexter Avenues until I finally found a milliner who was open. She cut a swatch of white veiling that looked something like cheesecloth, but it fulfilled the requirement. So we made sure they got married!"

Sara thought all the confusion, including a new snowstorm that began during the afternoon, added to the merriment of the day. And while she and Thelma waited in their bedroom for details like the rabbi and the saga of the veil to be settled, they discussed what Smithy's reaction would be when he saw Sara in a different dress, not the one he had picked out. "When my dad finally arrived to escort me into the living room, I walked in and saw Smithy's eyes," Sara remembers. "He was absolutely shocked that I wasn't wearing the dress he had chosen, and then, of course, he realized that Richard must have arrived with my dress. The look on his face was enough to keep me amused during the ceremony. Really, I don't think I heard one word that the rabbi said. I just wanted the ceremony to be finished. Very shortly I heard the rabbi asking Smithy to place the ring on my finger, and he pronounced us man and wife, and Smithy kissed me very lovingly and tenderly. Smithy then stepped on the glass, and everyone shouted *Mazel Tov, Mazel Tov*, and began hugging and kissing."

After a buffet dinner, the diminutive bride and groom changed their clothes, said goodbye to their families and friends and went off to their waiting 1939 Plymouth. All kinds of noisemakers and tin cans and "Just Married" signs were attached to the car. They drove to the Dearborn Inn, where they found a beautiful bouquet of flowers and a basket of fruit in their room.

"What a memorable night," Sara says. "My Smithy was so kind, so loving, gentle and considerate. I put on my nightgown and my negligee and we read some verses from the Bible. Then when we went to bed, I took off my negligee and we snuggled closely together. Remember, Smithy and I were both virgins. I didn't know what to expect, but Smithy must have done a lot of reading, for he seemed to know what to do. I was very frightened. My parents had never talked about sex to their children. In fact, when a pregnant woman came to visit, we had to leave the room. Also, there were no classes in school about sex, and I went around with girls who didn't talk about it. Strange but true. Anyway, Smithy was just so loving and considerate that the first night we just fell asleep in one another's arms.

"The next morning, we got up with such enthusiasm and joy, and we dressed in no time and went down for breakfast hand in hand. We called my family and Smithy's mother, and we expressed such happiness that I know we made my family very, very happy."

After the first four days of their honeymoon, Smithy and Sara met up with Smithy's best man and their dear friend Ben Chinitz, in Knoxville, Tennessee. Ben then traveled with them for the remainder of their honeymoon. This shared honeymoon had come about because the previous summer, Smithy and Ben had planned a vacation to the Smoky Mountains during spring vacation. Of course, Smithy hadn't realized he would be getting married, so when he and Sara set their date, Ben was disappointed that he and Smithy wouldn't be going on their trip. Ben also had been working very hard planning Purim festivities for the Sunday school, and he had gotten sick, but he just kept working. He really needed a vacation. When Sara told her sister Helen how Ben was feeling, Helen said, "Well, Sara, that boy needs help. Why don't you invite him to come along?"

"What? On our honeymoon?"

"Why not? You're going to be married on Thursday. You'll be gone Thursday, Friday, Saturday and Sunday by yourselves. Why couldn't Ben meet you on Monday at a convenient place? That might help him, and it wouldn't hurt you because you already would have had four days together."

Sara said, "I don't think that's a bad idea! I'll ask Smithy what he thinks."

Smithy thought it was a fine idea, and realized that if Ben came along, he also would be able to bring the movie camera he had ordered, which was arriving later than they'd expected. Ben was delighted, and immediately felt happier. "Look, you'll have a chauffeur!" he said. "You two can sit in the back of the car and I'll sit in front and be the driver."

So it was that Sara and Smithy traveled to Ohio and Kentucky and then on to Tennessee, where they met up with Ben Chinitz at the appointed time. The next day they started out for the Smoky Mountains, and had a wonderful time, stopping to look at all the beautiful scenery. At dinner one night, talking about the idea and institution of marriage, Ben told Smithy and Sara that he would like to get married, and that when they got back from this trip he wanted to find the girl he would marry.

"Why don't we pretend that you have your wife along with us?" Sara said. "We know she exists. You just don't know who she is yet, but this way we can get to know more about her."

"Of course we didn't know who she was, but we knew he was going to have a wife, and so we pretended she was there," Sara said. "I'll never forget one morning in the Smokies, when we stopped at the Grand Hotel and we were having breakfast. Smithy, Ben and I were all talking to this empty chair, asking Ben's pretend wife what she would like for breakfast. We were having such a jovial time, and then all of a sudden we looked up and there was the waitress, who must have been wondering what in the world was going on. We all became very subdued and quiet and ordered our breakfasts. When she left, we really burst into a lot of laughter. We had a great time. When we drove along, the three of us sang and sometimes we would take an opera and just use words like 'vanilla and chocolate ice cream' and just ramble along with those words to the melody of the operas."

When they got back, Sara's family hosted a reception for Smithy and Sara that included all of their friends who hadn't been able to be at the wedding. For the reception, Sara wore the dress that Smithy had picked out for her to wear at the wedding.

In the evening, after the reception, the two kissed their friends and family good night and went to Smithy's mother's home. They had planned to rent an apartment, but Smithy's brother Lou, who had been living at home but wanted to move to California, suggested that Smithy bring his bride back to live with Mother Smith. The Smith family decided it was a good idea, and so it was settled. Mother Smith was very happy to have the newlyweds, and even though initially it had been a blow for Sara and Smithy, who wanted their own place, it turned out to be a blessing for the year and a half that they lived there. "When we came home from teaching, dinner was prepared," Sara says. "And often, she would wash and iron our clothes and put them out on the bed. It was really great because I wasn't really the greatest of housekeepers. I didn't know how to cook or to wash or iron or keep house. I was always a girl who liked to work on the outside and I never really was a so-called housewife."

Summer came before they knew it. School was out, and soon it was time for Sara to go back to the Fresh Air camp. In the middle of June, Smithy drove her to camp, and neither of them was very pleased or happy about being separated. In fact, Sara says, it was the unhappiest summer of her life. Every Wednesday night, Smithy would pick her up and drive her home, where she could stay until Friday morning, when she had to be back at camp. He also would come to visit her at the camp on Sundays, the visiting day. "Oh, when Smithy would leave me, I was so lonesome and so sick at heart that I promised never to go back," Sara says. "Smithy was the same; he felt so badly. I called him every evening, and I wrote him a letter every morning."

One time, when Smithy was feeling very dejected about staying with his mother while Sara was at camp, he told Sara that he couldn't imagine that he ever was going to find a way of getting their Frank Lloyd Wright house. He felt so forlorn and impoverished, he was sure it would never happen. "Home was a very, very important issue to Smithy," Sara says. "He was longing for a Frank Lloyd Wright home, and when I was gone, he was dwelling even more on thoughts of this home that we didn't have." Sara, who believed that prayer could answer any problem, wrote Smithy a prayer about the Frank Lloyd Wright home they would someday have together. She wrote about it as if it already existed:

ALL ABOUT HOME
We both, dear, because of our sincere efforts, will be led
into the very rightest path. There's only one plan, and we
can follow it and hurt no man.
His child is here to serve and to bless all.
I can say with much security and confidence that I'm grateful
for the beautiful home that we have now. The home
that we have now is the only home that we shall ever have.
As we beautify our thoughts, so shall our home, in proportion
to our thoughts unfold. It is a beautiful adventure, dear, and we can
accept it as such. It is an adventure filled with anticipation and joy.

After Sara returned from camp that summer, of course, she and Smithy had no home of their own; they were still living with Mother Smith. But with Smithy's desire and Sara's affirmation that their home was established and only had to manifest itself, the two had set a course. For Smithy, Sara's prayer, and her deep belief in what was possible, had special significance. He saved her letter and used it, often saying the prayer out loud with Sara. Even 50 years later, Sara could close her eyes and repeat the prayer for her son and grandchildren, just as she and Smithy had recited it together over and again throughout their lives.

"It was a blessing to both of us," Sara says. "When I think about this prayer, it seems that I didn't even write it, but that I heard it and then put the words on paper. I knew that one day our home would unfold. But to think that in 1940, I was giving thanks for the home we didn't move into until May, 1950. Do you wonder that I have this belief in prayer?"

"God takes care of our supply," says Sara. "We have nothing to worry about. Our job is just to listen to God's voice and obey what he is telling us."

Chapter 8

OF SERENDIPITY AND
THE ROAD HOME

Smithy carefully selected sara's clothes, folded and packed them in the suitcase. He was systematic, precise, orderly, and it made sense for him not only to decide what clothes they should take, but to do all the packing. Sara didn't mind Smithy picking out her clothes; he was particular, and in her opinion, he had beautiful taste. She watched with pleasure and a growing excitement. It was June 1941, the beginning of their first full summer together. They'd have no separations, no Fresh Air camp, no teaching. As soon as Smithy finished packing, they were setting out for Banff and Lake Louise. All year, they had been dropping their loose change in a little piggy bank—and that was money they would use on their trips.

The first full year of Sara and Smithy's marriage had been crowded with friends, fun and work. As dedicated teachers, both labored over daily lesson preparations and volunteered for extra tasks at their schools. On weekends, they prepared for and taught Sunday school, where Sara still directed dramatic presentations and Smithy continued to supervise the Sunday school newspaper. In addition, Smithy had taken Ben Chinitz's place as the Sunday School's principal. Ben had come back from Sara and Smithy's honeymoon determined to find his own wife, and he soon had. Within weeks of returning from the trip, actually, he had discovered Lillian Goodfriend, another teacher at the Sunday School. Lillian, who served as a counselor at Fresh Air with Sara, had been there all along, and Ben had finally noticed. At the time, Lillian was a senior in high school, but it was clear to Ben that the smart, beautiful brunette was the one he'd been waiting for all the time. Sara and Smithy often ate dinner or went out for a movie with Ben and Lil and were delighted when the new couple set a wedding date of September 22. Of course Sara and Smithy planned to be there.

But on the 20th of September, Nathan Stein, who was in his early 70's, suddenly got very sick, and on the 21st, he died. It was a shock to the entire family. So instead of attending a wedding on September 22nd, Sara and Smithy attended her father's funeral.

Before and after her father's death, Sara spent a great deal of time with her mother and with her sister Thelma, Thelma's husband Leo, and their son Marvin. She also spent a lot of time with her sister Min, who was living on Elmhurst with her husband Isadore and their two children, Phyllis and Elaine. And when she couldn't get over to see them, she called them. She spent so much time talking to her family that Smithy sometimes commented, "You might just as well be home, you're on the phone talking to them so much!" But Sara continued her phone calls on a regular basis.

Although Sara and Smithy had missed Ben and Lil's wedding in September, they were able to join them on their honeymoon over the Christmas holidays. Ben and Lillian had purposely delayed their honeymoon because of Ben's teaching schedule, and they'd hoped that Sara and Smithy would come along. The route of their trip, starting with Cincinnati, Cumberland Falls, and Berea, Kentucky, was very similar to Smithy and Sara's, only this honeymoon was more leisurely because they had more time—nearly two weeks. After leaving the Smoky Mountains, they went to Washington, D.C., where they ate at wonderful restaurants and visited the White House, the Lincoln Memorial, the Washington Monument and the Jefferson Memorial. Then they headed for Miami Beach, where they soaked up the sun, saw a number of shows, did a lot of swimming in the ocean and walking on the sand. The couple had a movie camera along that recorded much of the spontaneity and fun of their trip, including a joyful Sara as she splashed in the surf of the Atlantic Ocean. In the film, she rollicks in the water in her black swimming suit and white cap and then runs through the low tides and up on the beach, toward the camera. As she runs, she snatches off her swimming cap and shakes out her short head of hair. Laughing, she grabs a stick and scratches huge letters in the sand: "I LOVE SMITHY!" As she draws the letters, waves begin to wash up over their edges, and Sara beams at the camera.

Soon, they were back at work at their schools. And when May rolled around, Smithy and Sara, after five more months of teaching, were ready for summer vacation and another adventure. This one they would take all by themselves. Smithy carefully planned every detail of their route. They drove through Kalamazoo and Muskegon, Michigan, and up along the Wisconsin River, which cuts through canyons of castellated rock, toward Wisconsin Dells, from where they would head still further north to Canada. Smithy had read up on the dells, a natural attraction created over thousands of years by the river cutting through soft lime-stone to a depth of 150 feet. As they traveled through the Upper and Lower Wisconsin Dells, Smithy told Sara the way that the 15 miles of soaring rock formations had been created. "The dells were beautiful, and we were quite impressed," Sara remembers. "But they had bill-boards all over the place that took away from the natural beauty and ruined the area as far as we were concerned."

When they were getting ready to leave the dells, Smithy noticed a small sign with an arrow pointing toward the west that said: "Detour Spring Green/Taliesin."

"Look, Sara, we must be near Spring Green," Smithy said. "Let's take a detour! Let's go there and see Taliesin."

"Smithy always saw everything first," Sara remembers. "We had no idea that we were in the area of Spring Green." Of course, the two of them took the detour with enthusiasm and excitement. They were surprised and pleased that they could actually have an opportunity to see the place where Frank Lloyd Wright and many of his students lived and worked. Smithy, of course, had read a lot about Taliesen, which Wright had built between 1911 and 1925.

"Taliesin," which means "Shining Brow," was a place that was, in fact, a shining example of the way that Wright brought buildings, the landscape and life into a harmonious unity. As they drove through an open gate and up a long steep slope, the first thing Sara and Smithy noticed was a dam and a waterfall, which they later learned was part of a water system that fed all of the pools and fountains on the land. The buildings, which seemed to be cut into the hillside, jutted out over steep slopes below and were complimented by terraces, stone seats, enclosed flower gardens unlike anything either Smithy or Sara had ever seen.

They looked around at the stone buildings and a setting that in fact was reminiscent of beautiful Italian villas like the Villa Medici in Fiesole, and felt a sense of awe that anything could be this beautiful and at the same time exude such a sense of being so comfortable.

"We got there around 7:00 p.m.," Sara says, "and it was still light. Taliesen had their own time. They didn't go along with the world. We got out of the car and just stood there looking at everything. You would have thought we were on "holy ground" the way Smithy was looking around in such awe of everything he saw. We could see down the pathway to the drafting room and workshop. We had seen pictures of this building, and there it was. Smithy said, 'Sara, one day we *are* going to have a home designed by Frank Lloyd Wright.'"

Right then, a young man from the fellowship appeared out of nowhere, it seemed, and said, "Oh, are you interested in Mr. Wright designing your home?"

Smithy said, "Oh yes, I have been for a long time. We don't intend to build the home right this minute, but in the future, we want Mr. Wright to make the plans for us."

"Would you like to see Mr. Wright?"

Smithy gasped, and he and Sara looked at each other with shock. "We were both flabbergasted," Sara said later. "Imagine getting to meet this genius!"

"Would that be possible?" Smithy asked. "If so, we would be delighted!"

"Well, it's almost dinner time, but he might still be in his studio," the young man said. "He may have gone to the dining room, but if he is there, maybe you will see him. Why don't I go and ask."

He jumped into his jeep and drove off. Within minutes, he was back. "Mr. Wright is there, and he said he would see you."

"We were so overcome that we hardly had enough strength to get into that car," Sara remembers. "But we hopped into the jeep and away to Mr. Wright's studio we drove. They weren't having dinner until 8 o'clock, and it was maybe 7:30 or so when we got out of the jeep and walked towards the studio. Both of us were overcome at the prospect of seeing Mr. Wright. But there he was, on the threshhold of his studio, standing with his arm outstretched, looking like a vision. He was dressed in white and looked impeccable from his white hair to his white shoes.

"He greeted us with a smile, and the first question he asked was, 'Do you have any children?'

"Smithy and I both smiled and Smithy said, 'We haven't been married very long, but we are planning to have a family.'

"Mr. Wright invited us into his studio, and he sat down at his desk and Smithy and I sat down on chairs near his desk, with Smithy being nearest to him. Smithy did all the talking. I was so overcome with the whole experience, so awed by it, that I didn't say anything. It was just a privilege to just sit there and look at that man.

"Smithy told him that it was his great desire to have him design a home for us, and then he said, 'You know, we don't have very much money, but I read that you designed a home for the journalist, Mr. Herbert Jacobs, for $5,000. Could you design a home for us for five thousand?'

"I did design Mr. Jacobs' home in Wisconsin for that amount," Mr. Wright said. "But you see, that was back in the early 30s—some ten years ago. Prices have gone up since then. I doubt if I could do that."

"Well, what about $8,000? Could you do it for that?"

"I think I might be able to manage it for about nine thousand, but let's not talk about money now. Let's talk about you and the things that interest you the most."

"Smithy told him that we loved the arts and we loved to entertain," Sara says. "And music. . . . We loved chamber music, and we had the idea that we would love to have small concerts and art shows in our home."

Conversation flowed, and Frank Lloyd Wright found out more about the Smiths and their ideas about life, their plans and hopes.

Toward the end of their visit, Frank Lloyd Wright asked them how many bedrooms they would want in their home. They said that two bedrooms would be fine, and perhaps if they could also have a small study, it could double as a guest bedroom. That question was the only one that Frank Lloyd Wright asked them specifically about the house. After further discussion, Wright said, "I would advise you to find a piece of property that nobody else wants. It should have a knoll or some slope to it, something that makes it interesting and unusual. Make sure it's not flat." He said that a piece of property nobody else wants usually has character and interesting elements to it. Men in the building business level hills and valleys to build their houses, but Frank Lloyd Wright built his houses into the landscape so that the home was married to the land.

"Now find your land, get a topographical sketch of it, send it to me, and I will design a home for you."

When the interview was over, Sara and Smithy thanked Wright profusely. He walked them to the door, and they were on their way. "I don't think there were ever any two happier people," Sara says. "We got into the car really in a daze, because never in our wildest dreams had we ever thought we would meet Mr. Wright so early in our lives! We were thrilled with the experience, and it was then that I began to realize that there is no such thing as coincidence. I believe that there is only one plan, and if we listen, we will be led in the right direction.

"You can imagine what we talked about on the rest of that trip. We stayed for a week in a little cabin at Medicine Lake in Glacier Park, and one night in the dining room, the actress Myrna Loy walked in. What a beautiful woman she was."

Sara and Smithy also climbed Mount Henry along with a number of dining room workers and a photographer and saw the sunset from the summit. They also visited Banff and Lake Louise, where they stayed at a place called Ghost Haunt and sang songs around a fireplace, before traveling at their leisure through the Black Hills of North Dakota.

When they headed home in August to get ready for school again, they were counting their blessings for being schoolteachers with the entire summer off. They recounted their memories of breakfasts with poached eggs and pancakes, songs around a fireplace, seeing Myrna

Loy and Mount Rushmore, the presidents' heads carved out of granite in the Black Hills. But the most thrilling part of their trip was meeting the great Frank Lloyd Wright. That chance encounter would change their lives forever.

"Every challenge is an opportunity," says Sara. "And our dear Father will show us the solutions for all our challenges. So we have nothing to worry about. We never have to be concerned. All we have to do is to listen, love and obey what we hear."

Chapter 9

A CHANGE OF PLANS

AFTER SCHOOL BEGAN AGAIN, Sara and Smithy looked forward to their weekend excursions, when they packed picnic lunches into the car and drove around undeveloped areas looking for their dream site. Frank Lloyd Wright had said that they should have at least an acre for their house. Though an acre of land in most of the places they looked was simply beyond their means, they were hopeful and determined.

Through those autumn months, of course, along with the war tunes they heard over the radio, they heard news from Europe of Hitler and Stalin, and news of the Germans invading Crete and later, Russia. They followed the reports when Churchill and President Franklin D. Roosevelt signed the Atlantic Charter and when the British Royal Air Force bombed Nuremberg. But nothing had prepared them or other Americans for the December day they came home from Sunday school, turned on the radio and heard the horrible and shocking news that the Japanese had bombed Pearl Harbor.

Realizing that the United States would soon declare war, Smithy was concerned. One day he confessed to Sara that in addition to his worries about the catastrophe the country was facing, he felt sure that if there was a war, that also would be the end of his Frank Lloyd Wright house. The following day, December 8, 1941, the U.S. and Britain declared war on Japan. Later, of course, the allies were also at war with Germany and Italy.

In February, Smithy was drafted into the U.S. Armed Forces. "Smithy thought about being a conscientious objector because he didn't believe in wars," Sara says, "but the more he thought about it, the more he decided he would have to go. 'We want peace and I'm going to do what I can to help,' he told me. I was really very proud of him, but I had such a sinking feeling. So many of the men who had gone in January never came back; it seemed as though many of them were killed off right away. Both of us had many, many unhappy moments. I don't know where my trust in God was, but I certainly wasn't practicing what I had been taught in Christian Science. I was filled with such fear of the unknown, of what might happen to Smithy."

The time for Smithy's departure came all too quickly. Oscar Genzler, a friend of Sara and Smithy's who had been a counselor at the Fresh Air camp, also had been drafted and was supposed to report to Army headquarters on the same day as Smithy. The Genzler family offered to give Sara a ride home after Smithy and Oscar shipped out. "Someone in my family drove us downtown for Smithy to report," Sara says. "They dropped us off and I spent every second with Smithy until he was called to leave. We didn't think that we would ever see one another again. Oh, it was so sad. We'd been married for such a short time. Well, we said goodbye, and off he went in the bus.

"When I rode home with the Genzlers, I tried to hold back, but once I broke into tears, I couldn't stop crying. I cried all the way home. I didn't want anyone to be at the house when I got there. Mother Smith was in Florida and I went into an empty house, which suited me just fine. I wouldn't allow anybody to stay with me, and I didn't want anyone around me. I was so sure I would never see Smithy again. The reports of so many men being killed were constant. I forgot all my theories about listening to Our Father-Mother-God. I was just caught up with this awful war and all the disastrous harm that was happening to our soldiers. I was so caught up with the negative that I wasn't listening to the still small voice within me."

Three days after Smithy had left for basic training, he called Sara to say that she could come to Battle Creek for the weekend. He said that after he had left her, he had cried all the way to Camp Custer, where he currently was staying. Camp Custer, near Battle Creek, was only a three-hour drive from Detroit.

"Smithy's brother Jack and his wife Marian were living in Battle Creek, and they made arrangements for me to stay with them," Sara recalls. "Well, of course when the family heard that he would be there over the weekend, Smithy's mother and sister and the rest of the family wanted to see him, so everybody came to Battle Creek to stay at Jack and Marian's home.

"The whole family got to Jack's on Friday night," says Sara. "When we arrived, Marian had prepared a beautiful buffet dinner. I wasn't at all interested in the food, but everyone else was. I was only interested in being with Smithy. But with the whole family there, everybody wanted Smithy's attention and we had very little time with one another. Sleeping quarters were all over the house and I did not have any moments alone with Smithy. I was certainly happy to be in his company and he was happy to be in mine, but we had no privacy at all.

"Sunday morning came much too fast, and parting again was sad, but Smithy said, 'I'll expect you next weekend. By all the signs, it looks as though I'll be here.' I was so excited, I couldn't wait for the weekend to arrive. I thought possibly the whole family would not want to go again and Smithy and I could have some time to ourselves."

But Thursday the telephone rang and it was Smithy. There would be no weekend rendezvous. "We're shipping out Friday morning and Heaven knows where we're going," Smithy said. "They didn't tell us. But wherever I arrive, or wherever I'm going to be sent, believe me, I'll get in touch with you if there's any possible way to do so."

"I know, darling," Sara responded. "Everything is going to work out." But when she hung up the phone, she was crestfallen. Again, she says, she seemed to lack faith and confidence. Every day she rushed home after school hoping for a phone call.

"Of course he couldn't call whenever he wanted to. He had to wait for permission," Sara says. "So many limitations were put on the soldiers. Everything was so secretive, and of course we understood why. I didn't hear from him for more than a week, and of course in my mind, he already had been shipped out of the country."

But finally Smithy called, and he was at Sheppard Field in Wichita Falls, Texas, where he was attached to the Air Force. He told Sara that it looked as if he would be there for a while. Sara asked if she could join him, but he pointed out that he was only making $21 a month, which wasn't enough for them to live on, so they would have to be patient. She should plan to keep teaching and to come to Texas to see him for Easter vacation, which was about a month away.

A month seemed a long time, but Sara decided that she would help the time pass by making Smithy a sweater vest. She had never knitted anything before, but she put her mind to the task and knitted him a khaki-colored sweater vest that didn't have one single mistake and was "perfectly beautiful." Everyone admired it, and while someone said it might be a little too large for Smithy, they agreed it looked perfect.

When Easter vacation arrived, Sara carefully packed the finished sweater into her bags and departed by train for Wichita Falls. "Smithy met me at the train station, and we were so happy to see one another," Sara says. "He had a weekend pass, so we were able to stay with each other at the hotel. We traveled there by public transportation, and the minute we got there, I opened my suitcase and showed him the beautiful sweater I had knitted for him. Well, he took it out and tried it on, and we both got hysterical laughing because the sweater was much, much too large for him. It came down below his knees. I said, 'Well, I'll take it back home and give it to the USO. I'm sure they'll be able to find some soldier who will be able to fit into that sweater.'

"We had such a good time together. We didn't even want to walk the streets of Wichita Falls; we just wanted to stay in that beautiful room and be with one another. We did go down to the dining room to have dinner, and when we were there, Smithy introduced me to one of his soldier friends and the friend's wife, who also came from Detroit.

On Monday Smithy had to go to work, but he had a pass each night to come home and stay with me until vacation was over. So during the day, I traveled around with his friend's wife. We became friends and thoroughly enjoyed each other's company. I also met the Christian Science chaplain and his wife, who were darling people. When our vacation ended, the parting was difficult because we knew we wouldn't see each other until June."

Back in Detroit, Sara threw herself into her teaching. She moved in with Thelma, Thelma's husband Leo, and their children, Marvin and their newborn baby girl, Carol. Sara and Thelma's mother, Annie Stein, also was staying with Thelma to help with the baby. The fun of being with family and the demands of teaching kept Sara from being as lonesome as she otherwise might have been.

When her teaching semester ended in June, Sara packed her bags again and headed for Texas, planning to stay for the summer. She arrived on a Saturday and she and Smithy went back to their hotel to stay the first night. The next day they began to look for an apartment where she could stay for the summer. "We found a darling little apartment, but the landlord refused to rent it to us since Smithy was only a private. We felt a little unhappy about it, but we said, well, things will work out. There will be the right place for us. We enjoyed the day and then we came back to the hotel and went to our room and enjoyed a beautiful evening together. About two o'clock in the morning, the telephone rang and Smithy was told to report immediately to the barracks. His outfit was being shipped out.

"What a blow! We had thought we were going to be together for the whole summer, but it wasn't to be. We had no idea where he was going this time. He told me to go to my sister Essie's home in Indianapolis and he would call me there as soon as he had permission to do so. He said, 'For heaven's sake, be patient, and I will be patient, too. You and I know that God's directing all this. And we know he's been giving us the best of care. That has been our experience, and He certainly isn't forsaking us now.' So we kissed each other goodbye and off he went.

"In the morning, I called the Christian Science chaplain I'd met, and he and his wife came over immediately and took me to their home and made reservations for me to go to Indianapolis. I had lunch with them and then they drove me to the train station and stayed with me until I got on the train. They were dear and precious people, and I so appreciated everything they did for me. But I never contacted them again and I have reproached myself many times for that."

When Sara arrived in Indianapolis, she had no idea where Smithy was or when she would hear from him, and she also found her sister, Essie, critically ill. "Essie and her husband, Meyer, and their two children, Arlene and David, were so sweet and so loving, but Essie was very ill," Sara remembers. "She had what they thought was an incurable dis-

ease and that she would never get well. It was devastating." Sara and
Essie's sister Helen arrived from Chicago to help take care of Essie and
the sisters commiserated with one another. "I was wondering when I
would hear from Smithy and I was so worried about my sister, I just
couldn't find a sense of peace," Sara recalls. "Again, I wasn't practicing
my beliefs, I really wasn't listening to what I knew was true. I had such
a devastating feeling that things just were not going to work out.

"But they did. About a week and a half later, Smithy called and said
his troop had been sent to Atlantic City, and he was on the top floor of
the Ambassador Hotel in the 'Honeymoon Suite.' Of course, they had
taken out all the furniture and replaced it with Army cots. I was so
happy to hear from him.

"He said, 'Sara, leave tomorrow morning, and I know I'll be able to
meet you. In the meantime, I'll find a place for us to live while you're
here for the summer.' I told him about Essie's condition and said, 'She's
so ill. She doesn't want me to go, and she has this very, very bad sick-
ness, and they don't expect her to live.'

"Smithy said, 'Sara, I don't know how long I'm going to be here. You
may never see me again either.' He explained that Atlantic City was
a shipping-off place, and he might not even be there when I arrived,
but we could take the chance. He told me to decide what was more
important.

"I said, 'Of course, dear, I'll come to Atlantic City, and I will leave right
away.' Well, my sister was rather distraught that I was leaving, and so was
my sister Helen. But what could I do? I told them that Atlantic City was
a shipping-off point, so they could understand why I wanted to leave."

The following morning, Sara was on the train to Atlantic City. When
she arrived, Smithy met her at the station. He had rented a room for
them on the third floor of a small cottage that was right across the street
from a Christian Science church. The landlady, who realized that Sara
and Smithy didn't have much money for going out to eat in restaurants,
let them use her refrigerator for storing their food—mainly fruit, cottage
cheese and other things they didn't have to cook. Smithy was put on
permanent duty in Atlantic City, and they settled in.

When Smithy's mother and sister Jennie came for a visit, they took a room in the cottage for a week and took Sara and Smithy to lunch and dinner quite often. Thelma also came with Sara Horowitz and stayed for a week, as did Smithy's brother Marty, who was a dentist with the Coast Guard. Sara and Smithy enjoyed showing their family members around, going out on the town and walking down the Boardwalk.

"We had a wonderful time that summer," Sara remembers. "We went to U.S.O. shows, which were always free, but just being in Atlantic City was great. One evening when we were walking underneath the boardwalk, we stopped for a hug and a kiss, and when we were kissing, a policewoman approached us. 'What are you doing down here under the boardwalk?' she asked. She was very cross and accused me of being a whore, but Smithy said we were married and showed his identification. She became much gentler, but warned us never to walk under the boardwalk again, that it was too dangerous. After she left, we were highly amused, but we certainly went up and walked on top after that."

"The saddest thing was that I never did see my sister, Essie, again. She went to the Mayo Clinic, and she passed away there."

In September, Sara went back to Detroit to teach, but she was still uneasy about the possibility, no matter how remote, that Smithy would be shipped out. In November, however, Smithy came home for Thanksgiving weekend. "It was just a joy to have him with me in my arms," Sara says. We stayed at Thelma's and he was there Thursday, Friday and Saturday. He had to leave Sunday morning to drive back to Atlantic City by Monday. But before he left, he said, 'Sara, I think I'm going to have a wonderful surprise for you, but I can't tell you now. If it doesn't work out, I don't want you to be disappointed. Just be patient and wait. I'll call you Sunday night, because by that time, I'll know.'

Sara, pleading to know the secret, finally agreed to be patient and watched Smithy drive away in his Plymouth. She waited all week, and on the following Sunday night Smithy called Sara with good news. He'd passed a series of tests to become a Warrant Officer. Earlier, he had been given two offers: he could go to the Officer's Candidate School or he could take the Warrant Officer's test. If he had wanted a career in the Armed Forces, he said, he would have gone for the first option, but since he planned to leave the service as soon as the war was over, he'd chosen the second. The fact that he'd passed the test meant that he would be an officer and he would get a salary equivalent to a Second Lieutenant's, which meant that they could afford to have Sara join him in Atlantic City. "Sara, we'll be able to live in style!" he said. Smithy wanted her to take a leave-of-absence from teaching and join him during Christmas vacation, right after she had directed the Christmas program at her school.

On the first day back at school after the Thanksgiving break had ended, Sara went into school to tell her principal, Miss Redkey, that she had good news: she would be leaving soon. In fact, she would take a leave-of-absence that would start at the beginning of Christmas vacation, and continue through the spring.

Sara's relationship with her principal was complex. The previous year, Sara had been promoted to "auditorium" at Esterbrook School to replace a teacher who had moved to Florida. Auditorium was a class period during which students had the opportunity to learn the teacher's specialty and because of Sara's background and interest in the theater, she carried on a performing arts program during each of her auditorium sessions.

This was a tall order, however, because 80 children filed into the auditorium every 50 minutes. Sara, trying to maintain some order, put the 80 children into groups on the stage. The principal who gave her the promotion had told Sara not to worry about discipline, that she would be there to assist her in every way. But that principal was transferred to another school and was replaced by Miss Redkey, who became Esterbrook's principal—and Sara's nemesis.

"I had a very hard time with discipline," Sara says. "Often when I would put them into this group work, I'd see some of them running about on the floor, and I didn't have all the control I should have. This very much displeased Miss Redkey." Eventually, Miss Redkey called in the Regional Superintendent and said that she thought Sara should be transferred back to teaching kindergarten. But Sara objected. "As much as I used to love kindergarten, I do not want to go back there," Sara said. "I want to be given a chance to work out a performing arts program in this auditorium!"

After the meeting, Sara continued to teach auditorium, and Miss Redkey continued to be displeased. "Oh, I tried so hard, and I didn't seem able to do it," Sara says. "Well, Miss Redky then called in someone from the Board of Education to talk to me, and I told them I still wanted time. Miss Redkey said it was upsetting the whole school, and she thought I should move back into a situation where I had been successful. But the last period of the morning and the last period of the afternoon, I had 40 eighth graders. Forty wasn't 80, and I was able to manage those two groups very well. At the time, this morning group was working on a play about Rip Van Winkle. We had great lighting and a great stage crew, and the eighth graders were very receptive to what I had to offer them.

"As we were rehearsing one morning, someone came in and sat down and watched me with this particular group. I looked up and saw that it was Dr. Miriam Edmond, the supervisor of the auditorium for the Board of Education. But you know, I didn't pay her any mind. I just kept on with the show. All the children were interested in what they were doing, and when we got to the end of the rehearsal, there were all sorts of claps and 'Bravo!' from Dr. Edmond. She came up and shook hands with me and said, 'You are doing a positively magnificent job! I don't know when I have seen a rehearsal of *Rip Van Winkle* as well as you have done it. Your lighting, technical work, acting, stage decorations—they're just beautiful!'

"That was certainly a different response from the feedback I'd been hearing. Well, then Dr. Edmond and I walked into Miss Redkey's office, and Dr. Edmond said, 'You have a wonderful auditorium teacher here; she's exceptional! Do you know your trouble, Miss Redkey? Your difficulty is that you have given this young teacher a situation that should be handled by two auditorium teachers.'"

The very next morning, another teacher showed up to share the work load with Sara. They began to alternate periods, with each of them teaching one 50-minute period with the help of the other. "I had a wonderful time teaching every other 50-minute session," Sara says. "The two of us got along very well, and it worked out beautifully. We invited the Board of Education to one program we whipped up for a special anniversary, and Miss Redkey was so proud. She thought we were the greatest."

So, when Sara told Miss Redkey that she was leaving to join her husband in Atlantic City, Miss Redkey was quite distressed. "Sara, you've done a terrific job in this auditorium," Miss Redkey said. "I'll be very sorry to see you leave."

Following the successful Christmas show that Sara mounted with the students, Miss Redkey and the teaching staff gave Sara a going-away luncheon, presenting her with an orchid corsage and a book, *Treasures in Poetry*.

When classes ended for Christmas vacation, Smithy's family took Sara to the train station in Detroit, where, wearing the orchid corsage on the shoulder of a mink coat she had previously purchased, she boarded the night train to Atlantic City and her new life. In the morning, she stepped off the train and was embraced by her husband, in an officer's uniform and long black wool military coat, who ran toward her with outstretched arms.

"I guess I did look lovely," Sara says. "At least Smithy told me how ravishing I looked. And how handsome he looked in his officer's uniform and coat! As the two of us walked arm-in-arm over to his car, noncommissioned officers would salute him and he constantly was saluting back, and he would nudge me and I would nudge him. We were highly amused, you know, at this different atmosphere that was created by Smithy being an officer."

"The minute we worry or get upset," Sara says, "we are not trusting God."

Chapter 10

WE'RE IN THE ARMY NOW

Until she became an army wife, Sara had never actually taken care of a house, cooked meals or done laundry. Smithy's mother had done their washing, ironing and cooking when they lived with her, and in Thelma's house and her own mother's house, Sara had been the helper, not the woman in charge.

The previous summer in Atlantic City, Sara had served meals by carrying cold food on a tray from the landlord's refrigerator up to their room. But now, for better or worse, Sara was head of household. Their new apartment had a stove with an oven, so Sara faced a serious challenge—cooking. But cooking never would really capture her imagination. "I was just the kind of person who liked to work and to do things outside the home," she later said. "I wasn't a lot for housekeeping." Nevertheless, in Sara and Smithy's small apartment, along with the living room, bedroom and kitchen, came an area called a "dinette," and Sara was determined to use it.

"I wasn't the greatest of cooks," Sara says in what other family members laughingly say is a dramatic understatement. "But I had an opportunity to practice cooking in this particular kitchen, and I had fun experimenting there. I made one dish that Smithy liked very much. It was vegetable spaghetti, and I used creativity and originality in making it. I didn't follow a recipe. I just put all kinds of vegetables in it—peas and tomatoes, mushrooms, celery and green peppers. Well, Smithy loved that particular dish."

An experiment that didn't go quite as well as vegetable spaghetti was the steak that Sara cooked one night when they had a couple over for dinner. "I prepared this dinner, and I put the steak into the broiler when they arrived. But when we sat down to eat our meal, the steak was as raw as it could be. I didn't allow nearly enough time for cooking it. We all laughed about it, and we put it back into the broiler over and over again until it was finally edible."

Another interesting cooking experience for Sara came on Smithy's birthday, March 12th, when Sara decided to bake him a cake. They planned to go out for dinner and have the birthday cake upon their return. "I made him a seven-layer cake," Sara says, "and each layer had all this beautiful chocolate icing. But it was as heavy as lead. I think if I would have thrown it at anyone, it would have knocked them out. I knew we wouldn't be able to eat that cake—we just wouldn't. Well, I certainly played into luck's hand that evening because we went out for such a big dinner, and then we went to the theater, and after the theater, we ate ice cream sundaes, so by the time we got home, neither one of us was hungry. The caked *looked* beautiful, so Smithy said, 'We'll have it tomorrow night.' That pleased me because I knew we would never be able to eat that cake. And the next day when I brought it out, we really laughed about it. Smithy had a good sense of humor, and we were laughing when we threw it into the rubbish."

Sara's Aunt Rose visited Sara and Smithy in Atlantic City, and her visit was followed by one from Thelma, her son Marvin, and Annie Stein, who had come again to see her daughter. Sara loved having her family there. During another visit from her mother and Thelma in the late spring, Smithy received notice that he was being transferred to Goldsborough, North Carolina. At the time, Sara was about two months pregnant, which her family did not yet know. Smithy urged Sara to go back to Detroit with her sister and mother and to let him get settled in Goldsborough before she joined him there. He gave her a long lecture about being careful, not lifting anything, and taking good care of herself. He never learned that when Sara, her sister and mother got on the train back to Detroit, all the seats were filled, and they had to stand most of the way. "The trip took its toll on me," Sara remembers. "I didn't feel that great."

About three weeks later, Smithy got permission for a leave to pick

Sara up in Detroit and to drive her back with him to North Carolina. "I was so grateful to see him in that beautiful old Plymouth of his," Sara says. "We were going to repeat the route we took on our honeymoon, going to Cincinnati and through the Smoky Mountains. When we got to the Smoky Mountains, we stayed at a little cabin way up in the mountains, away from everything. That night I started to contract and I lost that little baby. I didn't go to the doctor. Smithy and I just worked it out together, and there was nothing we could do about it. But Smithy was so loving and tender, and so careful with me that I was able to travel. I wasn't all that comfortable, but I did manage to make it, and we arrived in Goldsborough and spent a few nights at a hotel until finally we were able to get into our little nest."

This nest, a studio apartment in a newly finished Army project, had a large living room with an adjacent dining room. The living room couch, more like a cot, opened up into a bed for two, and they cooked on a coal stove. Coal stoves were hard to light, and most of the wives in the apartment complex were "city girls" like Sara, who didn't know anything about coal stoves. "One girl, Nancy, always seemed to manage to get her stove started early in the mornings," says Sara. "And so all the girls would run to her stove with their coffeepots. I have to laugh when I think of her. She was such a trooper! Smithy and I didn't drink coffee, but I would go with my kettle to boil water so Smithy could have something hot to drink."

Sara remembers the experience of living in that complex with the other Army wives as particularly delightful. They were all young, recently married women, and the fact that they were geographically removed from their families, and both frightened and exhilarated by the war, gave them an instant and intimate connection with one another. Also, being personally linked to the ever-present threat of separation and death gave them a heightened sense of being alive. At a moment's notice, the Army could ship out their husbands, and once gone, who could say whether they'd ever return. The husband of one of Sara's friends came home one morning and told his wife and two-year-old son that he had to leave in two hours. "That's just the way they did things in the Army," Sara recalls. "They wouldn't give you any time at all. That was my fear—that Smithy would be shipped out. I always lived with that fear. Again, not practicing my faith."

The women, on their own during the days, supported each other by sharing supplies and tips and small and large acts of kindness. The chaplain's wife, who had diabetes and couldn't eat anything with sugar, for instance, baked cakes and cookies for the other women. "She was so happy to have other people enjoy her baking," Sara says. "What an unselfish girl she was!" Sara became especially close friends with the woman who lived next door, Sylvia, whose husband was the musical director and bandleader for the camp. "They had a hi-fi, and the four of us used to spend our evenings listening to recordings," Sara says. "Smithy just loved music, and he and the bandleader spent a lot of time together, too."

While living in that complex in Goldsborough, North Carolina, Sara got pregnant for the second time. "I went to the doctor and told him about the experience I'd had in the Smoky Mountains, and he said he thought it would be best to stay in bed for at least the next two months and take it easy until I was well set with this baby. So I did. We were careful and did what the doctor told us to do. Smithy was very concerned about my lifting or picking anything up, and he would ask me what I would need at noontime and then he would leave everything out on the counter so I wouldn't have to bend over. He did everything for me. And the girls would come in and help me out, too. Everybody was so loving and helpful, and we managed along very nicely because we didn't want to lose this baby!" Sara made it successfully through the first three months of her pregnancy, and then she was able to stay up and move around freely again.

When Sara was about five month's pregnant, Smithy's boss, Colonel Jones, suggested that in her condition, Sara shouldn't be living in that little project. He suggested that Smithy rent a house for Sara, and he happened to know of one right across the street from where he lived. Smithy agreed. The colonel helped Smithy rent furniture for the place—which looked to Sara "like a little doll house"—and Sara and Smithy moved in. "The colonel's wife was right across the street," Sara says, "and she was very kind and helpful, but it wasn't as much fun as the project because I was more or less alone. There weren't too many homes around there, but I made myself happy because Smithy would come home for lunch and for dinner."

One day Smithy came home and told her that two of his superior officers wanted to come over for dinner. They were from New York, and they missed home-cooked meals. One of the officers particularly loved and longed for a lemon meringue pie. The announcement threw Sara into a panic. "Of course, with officers coming to our house, I had to make an entire meal," she says. "Also, since this one man really wanted a home-baked pie, I was bound and determined to make him one. Of course, I didn't know one thing about making a pie. And I didn't know one thing about making a pie crust either, so I called my friend Nancy and told her I didn't have any dough to make the crust. She said she'd bring me over some Crisco and I could make the crust with that. At the time Crisco was rationed and a very hard item to get, but Nancy came to my rescue and brought me some.

"I must have put too much Crisco into the pie dough, though, because the dough wouldn't turn into crust. It had liquid running out of it everywhere, and I couldn't use it at all. I had to throw it away. So I called Colonel Jones' wife and told her my dilemma, and she said, 'Don't worry, Sara. I have a Flako crust that you can have. All you have to do is to put it in a pie pan, put it in the oven, and it will be just perfect.' I thanked her profusely because I thought that would be great! The minutes were turning into hours and I was nowhere close to starting dinner. But I had to get the pie made, so I started making the lemon custard. I don't know what happened, but I just couldn't get the lemon custard to thicken. It remained all watery, and I knew I couldn't use it, so I just threw it down the drain.

"I thought, Oh good heavens, I have this beautiful crust, but I don't have a filling! And then I realized I had some chocolate pudding. I could make a chocolate pie! So I made chocolate custard and put it in the pie shell. When that was done, I knew I should have a covering, and I took some whites of eggs and beat them up and put the meringue over the pie. If nothing else, at least we would have a chocolate pie.

"Well, of course, bothering so much with this pie, I didn't have very much time to make the dinner! Smithy had done the shopping at the commissary. They had wonderful food there, much less expensive than the commercial food you would buy in a store, and he had bought a very thick steak roast. I didn't put the roast in as early as I should have, but I put it in the oven. When I put it in, I forgot about baking the potatoes, and later it dawned on me, Oh, you have to have baked potatoes! So I quickly peeled the potatoes and put them in with the steak roast, and then I made a salad. I was always good at making salads.

"Well, my guests arrived and I was very happy to see them, but I wasn't too secure about my dinner. When I saw them, I remembered I had forgotten to cook the string beans, so I put them on to cook. I also knew that the roast should probably have cooked at least another hour. I felt the potatoes and they were almost as hard as rocks, so I tried to stall dinner for a little while, but I couldn't stall for too long. If only I had prepared some hors d'oeuvres and had something to drink, we could have sat for at least a half-hour, but I just hadn't planned it all out. Well, anyway, they arrived, and we greeted them and then we had some champagne. After I had stalled as much as I could, Smithy said, 'Well honey, aren't we ready to sit down yet?'

"I was not the slightest bit ready, but I said, 'Yes, of course!' We all sat down at the table and Smithy helped me with the salad and the bread and butter. We took quite a little while eating the salad. I ate very slowly, much too slowly in fact, but this was just to give me a few more extra minutes. I kept stalling, but finally Smithy said, 'Sara, isn't it time to serve our main dish now?'

"I said, 'Oh yes, of course!'"

"So we took off the salad plates and got the roast out of the oven. Smithy got out the carving knife and started trying to cut the roast, and you could tell it wasn't done because he worked so hard at it. He was a little concerned because he knew it wasn't cooked enough, but he sliced it and put a slice on each dish and then served the potatoes. It's a good thing he didn't put his fork in the potatoes, because he would have bent the fork. The roast, sad to say, you had to practically saw it, and it took a lot of energy. I just said to myself, 'Good luck, people!'

"They seemed to manage to eat it, but they certainly had to chew very, very slowly. I was truly very embarrassed by that dinner, but nobody seemed to complain. One of the potatoes did slip off the plate because this boy's fork wouldn't go into it. But he just picked it up and put it back on his plate.

"Anyway, we managed. We got through the main meal and we laughed and talked, and after we'd eaten, Smithy cleared the table and put the dishes in the sink. When I took out the pie, it looked like a lemon meringue pie, and this boy said, 'Oh, I hear you make the best lemon meringue pies!' I told them that my lemon pie just hadn't worked out, but I had made a chocolate pie, and he said, 'Chocolate pie! That's one of my favorite pies. I love chocolate pie!' And the pie really was delicious, and we drank coffee and continued talking. So when it was time to bid adieu and they left, they said what a good dinner I had prepared, but really, they were being very gracious about the whole thing.

"After they took off, Smithy cleaned up and he said, 'Now Sara, don't worry about the dinner. I know the meat was really tough and the potatoes were too hard, but you haven't had any experience making dinners.' He was very kind about it, but that was the last dinner during the service where I invited anybody over. Girls from the project would come over to lunch every once in a while, but oh heavens, I tried to stay away from making dinners. I seemed to be able to cook all right for Smithy—or at least he pretended to be satisfied with what I prepared. But we had a great time just being together and counting our blessings."

In May, everything changed. Smithy received orders to transfer to Gulfport, Mississippi, another shipping-out station, and Sara was sure that Smithy was about to be sent off to other parts of the world, and that their life together would come to an end. By then Sara was in her seventh month of pregnancy and Smithy felt she should go back to Detroit to have the baby. She wanted to go to Gulfport with him, but he was concerned about conditions in Gulfport. He wanted her to have a good obstetrician and to have support when she had the baby. "What if we go to Gulfport and then I get shipped out?" he asked her. "What would you do there expecting a baby and knowing absolutely no one in town?"

So in May of 1944, Sara took the long train ride back to Detroit and moved in with Thelma and Leo and NooNoo (Marvin). "As the days went on, it got warmer and warmer, and I got larger and larger," Sara says. "It was one of the hottest summers that Detroit had had in a long while. The baby was supposed to have been born in June, but somehow or other, he was a little stubborn, and it got to be July and the baby still hadn't come. Smithy was upset because he constantly thought he was going to be sent off to foreign lands, and I did, too. I thought my world would end, but that didn't happen.

"Thelma was an absolute angel. She didn't leave my side for over two months. We were like Siamese twins. And as May and June went by, Smithy stayed in Gulfport. Then he was transferred to Biloxi, Mississippi, but since he was still in the country, we were happy about that.

"I was getting signals that it was time for the baby to arrive, and then my water burst, so we went to the hospital, but after several hours, nothing had happened. Thelma and Leo were with me, and finally the doctor sent me home. We waited until the contractions started coming, and then we went back to the hospital. I was in such pain that I just screamed. I had never had pain like that in my whole life. One doctor, who was unsympathetic and cold, said, 'Hey, tell that girl to keep quiet.' Boy, did that nurse give it to him. She said, 'You don't know what it's like. You never had a baby!' At that time, there weren't needles you could take or medicine, and I truly suffered.

"I suffered so much that I never wanted to have another child. Thelma and her husband stayed right by my side, and the labor went on and on and on. The baby's head wasn't in the proper place, and they thought they would have to do a cesarean, so I called up my practitioner, Marion Reading, and do you know, after I talked to her, and after she prayed and worked with me, the baby turned around and came out normally. My son Bobby was huge—he weighed 9 pounds, 3 ounces and was 21 inches long at birth.

"After he was born, they did let me hold him for a few seconds, but then they took me back to my room. Very shortly after that, they brought him to me again. His head came up to a point from the use of forceps to get him out, and he had the blackest hair that you could ever imagine—pitch black and real long and stringy. And his cheeks were all red because they had methylate on them. What a *wonderful* experience it was to hold that little baby! Bobby was so beautiful! I did try to nurse him, but evidently my milk wasn't that great because he started losing weight. So they put him on a formula and then he was all right."

Sara had complications from the birth, and they kept her in the hospital for more than a week. When she finally went home from the hospital, she took her baby with her, and initially they stayed with Thelma and her family. "My mother and Smithy's mother came over and helped take care of Bobby," Sara says. "I couldn't get out of bed at the time, and the two mothers would diaper Bobby, and each one would tell the other one how to do it. It was humorous watching the two of them!"

Sara's niece, Phyllis Clinton, then a newlywed, remembers the time vividly. "After the baby was born, Sara really wasn't well," Phyllis later said. "He was a big baby for such a little woman. I mean, she was always tiny. And she was in labor for a long time. She should have had a caesarian, not natural birth. He should have been taken out. Afterwards she was very sick for a long time.

"At first she was at Thelma's with the baby, but Thelma's husband was a milkman, and he had to get up in the middle of the night to get to work. But Bobby used to cry and he kept Leo up, so my mother Minnie says, 'Come to our house!' Now my dad had rheumatoid arthritis very badly. They didn't know what it was in those days, but it started in his legs. Eventually he was able to walk, but he was so out of shape and always in pain. "Anyway, we just had a one-bedroom apartment, but it had the kind of bed that comes out of the wall. So my dad and mom took the Murphy bed in the living room, and Sara and the baby had the bedroom. She was like a washed-out dishrag for a long time. I used to go to the apartment, and I'd say, 'Mom, how long can this go on?' But it went on a long time, and that was our family. They helped each other.

"Also, Sara was so sweet and good and kind. She never talked bad about anybody and she never complained. All the Stein girls were that way. You know that saying, 'If you can't say something nice, don't say anything at all?' They always lived by that motto."

When Smithy got a one-week leave, they had a *bris*, the Jewish ceremony to keep the covenant of circumcision and to celebrate the child. "Smithy was right there with me for the full week," Sara says. "It was so sad when he had to leave because we were always afraid that he would be shipped out. I couldn't help the fears that grabbed hold of me. Even with my philosophy, fear just took over and played havoc with me.

"I stayed in Detroit for three months because I really wasn't able to travel, and Smithy wasn't able to find a place. During the war time, living conditions at a base were very bad. But we talked all the time on the phone, and after three months I said to Smithy, 'Well, even if you don't find a place, I'm coming anyway.'"

When it was time to leave Detroit, Smithy's sister Jennie and her husband took Sara and Bobby to the train station. Sara had Bobby in a bassinet, and Jen and Irv settled them on the train to Mississippi. In Biloxi, Smithy met them at the station. "He had found us a place where we could only have kitchen privileges to heat the baby's bottle," says Sara. "Otherwise we were not allowed in the kitchen. The owner did allow me to do washing outside in tubs, which wasn't very convenient, but that was the situation.

"One day this woman we rented the room from said, 'Sara, I've decided that you can have the use of the home and the kitchen. You can use this home as your own home.' We had a nice friendly relationship, and I was so pleased. When Smithy came home, I told him, and he said, 'No, Sara, I don't want to stay here. I want to find my own place, and I'm going to keep looking. You can just tell her that when we find a place, we'll move out.' When I told her that, she was so upset to think that I would refuse her offer. When Smithy came home and brought me my lunch or dinner, she would sit on the couch and look daggers at Smithy before he and I went on up to our room to eat. Eventually Smithy did find a place, a darling place. Some woman had built log cabins for officers, and he found this one log cabin and we moved into it."

In their log cabin, Sara and Smithy were housed near other officers and their wives. Sara found a good friend in one woman who had a little girl the same age as Bobby. "Every morning she would take one hour off while I'd take care of her baby and my baby, and then I would have an hour off and she would take care of the two children," Sara says. "It's amazing how much you can get done in an hour when you don't have to keep watching your child.

"Then we'd both have lunch in our own homes and put the babies down for their naps. After the babies woke up, we would take a walk down to the water. We had a great companionship. Our husbands weren't that friendly, so we just saw one another during the day."

Life was just beginning to seem rather idyllic when Smithy got orders to transfer to Fort Worth, Texas, where he would still work in the Intelligence Division on a cumulative history of the war. "When they tell you you're going to be transferred, you move so fast you don't even have time to say good-bye to the people you love," says Sara. "You have an hour or two to get ready to leave. With this girl, I never did get a chance to get her home address. I was just able to say goodbye and run. Isn't that a shame? But it's the Army."

In Fort Worth, Sara, Smithy and Bobby lived in a motor lodge that had been turned into a military housing complex. Lots of other Army families lived nearby, and one of the small but significant pleasures was a nearby watermelon stand, where the watermelons were orange, not red, and extraordinarily sweet. For Bobby's first birthday, Sara and Smithy bought a birthday cake and ice cream and invited all the nearby Army children and their parents for a party. "We had a great time, with one exception," Sara remembers. "Bobby was sleeping, and we had to wake him up for the party, and he cried all the way through it. We just couldn't get him to stop crying. So it wasn't all that successful, but we did manage to at least have a party! I can still see him at the party—teary-eyed, but so darling."

On weekends, Smithy, Sara and Bobby spent a lot of time at the zoo and walking through beautiful local gardens and parks. It wasn't long before Bobby was walking and excitedly pointing to bright flowers and bushes. He was thrilled by the bears, lions and monkeys he saw at the zoo. By then, the black hair Bobby had been born with had been replaced by a golden shade of curls and ringlets. Sara, playful and full of ideas, had fun taking her golden-haired child on adventures during the day. She loved reading to him and watching him as he discovered himself and the world around him.

"I've learned that everybody's wonderful. God never created evil; he only created good. We have to accept that everybody is wonderful and perfect. Sometimes it isn't easy to see that. Sometimes we're challenged. But if we stick with it, it works."

—Sara Stein Smith

Chapter 11

AFTER THE WAR:
The Search Continues

IN EARLY AUGUST, 1945, the United States dropped bombs on Hiroshima and Nagasaki, and on August 14, 1945, Japan surrendered, ending World War II. Deaths from World War II military actions were estimated at 35 million. An additional ten million people—Jews, homosexuals, gypsies, handicapped persons, as well as Christians and others who actively opposed Hitler or were caught working for the Resistance movement—had been murdered in Nazi concentration camps.

The idea of peace was wonderful, yet shocking and confusing. Once again, in what seemed like an instant, life changed dramatically. The relief of the war ending, as well as the grief and the joy of having survived, combined to create an extraordinary camaraderie among strangers, a promise of rebuilding lives and families, and an almost giddy optimism about the future.

For Sara and Smithy, the end of the war meant a return to Detroit, a return to teaching, a return to their families and friends, and a resumption of optimistic living. It also meant the revival of Smithy's deep and abiding, but for the time, submerged, dream of building a Frank Lloyd Wright house. To others, it must have seemed pure fantasy, pie in the sky. But Smithy and Sara, with an almost dream-like confidence, believed it still could happen. After all, hadn't Mr. Wright promised that *when* they found their land, he would design their house? Now, with the war over and Smithy safe, it still could happen. They reminded themselves out loud that when they had saved enough money and when they found the land, they would buy it. Then, Frank Lloyd

Wright would design their home, just as he had promised. It was true that they had very little money. But they had each other and they had their dream.

They were in high spirits when they packed their car and headed for St. Louis, where Smithy got his discharge. Then it was back to Detroit, where they stayed first with Sara's sister, Thelma, and then with Minnie. Minnie and Isadore gave Sara and Smithy their bedroom and slept in the living room. "We were crowding them out," Sara says, "and I said to Smithy, 'Why don't you ask Jennie if we can stay there?'" Smithy's sister Jennie, who had an enormous home, was equally welcoming. So Sara and Smithy moved with Bobby and his little crib into Jennie and Irv's master bedroom.

"It was huge and mirrored and lovely," Sara says. "We loved it—and Jennie loved having us there." Soon after they moved in, Smithy's brother Marty, who had been stationed in New Orleans, brought his new bride, Marjorie, home to Jennie's third floor. Marjorie and Sara became very close friends and spent a lot of time together. When Mother Smith came back from a stay in Florida, she, too, lived with Jennie and her family.

"There was quite a houseful," Sara says. "We did a lot of entertaining, and people came and went all the time." Since they had returned to Detroit, Smithy was busy teaching and Sara was enjoying staying at home with Bobby, playing with him and going out on adventures with him and her nieces and nephews. Staying at Jennie's house became a problem for Sara and Marjorie, however. Having all those people in the house was too big a job for Jennie—but she would never allow Sara, Marjorie or anyone else to come into the kitchen or help with the work. She wouldn't allow them to shop or to contribute in any way to the running of the household. "They had help, but not being allowed to do anything made me uncomfortable," Sara says. "I didn't care for that. In May, I told Smithy, 'When June comes, I can't stay here any longer. I want a place of our own.'"

"What will you do if we can't find a place?" Smithy asked.

"I don't care. We'll just get into the car and travel around like gypsies, as far as I'm concerned."

Finding a place to live wouldn't be easy. The post-war housing market was booming, and empty apartments were scarce. Soldiers coming back from the war were moving to new jobs and new schools. The war had changed things; more people than ever before were in transit to new locales. Now it was virtually impossible to get a house, and the only way to get an apartment was to give the superintendent of a building a couple of thousand dollars in "key" money. Sara and Smithy, who were saving every extra penny to put into their Frank Lloyd Wright home, weren't about to pay bribe money for a place to live.

With a little help from their friends, however, they got lucky. Sara's sister Helen had a sister-in-law, Ann Ross, who worked for the city and thought she might be able to secure a place for them in a project called Herman Gardens. Herman Gardens, built for people with low incomes, was filled with soldiers and their families. "Ann pulled some strings and was able to get us a little apartment there," Sara says. "So Smithy and Bobby and I moved in there at the end of June, right after school ended.

"It was small and the floors were all cement, but you can make a home wherever you are, and if you love it, the conditions don't make any difference. We made ourselves very comfortable. We borrowed a sofa bed from Mother Smith, and we borrowed kitchen chairs and a kitchen table. We just didn't want to invest any money in furniture, because we knew we wouldn't be living there too long."

All of the Smiths have happy memories of Herman Gardens. On Bobby's second birthday, they had a party attended by both of their families. "We bought a beautiful cake and put the candles on it," says Sara, laughing at the memory. "It was on the kitchen table, and so much was going on that we weren't watching Bobby too closely. He was so curious about the cake that he went into the kitchen, climbed onto a chair and pulled the cake toward him. He loved icing, and he wanted to taste some of it. He was bound and determined that he was going to get that icing, but he didn't get very much of it. The cake fell on the floor and got all over him, and it was so funny. Smithy picked the cake up and plastered it back together on the plate and it looked like nothing had happened. We sang 'Happy Birthday!'"

On weekends, Sara and Smithy packed Bobby and picnic lunches in their car and once again started venturing out, driving around the suburbs of Detroit to look for property—just as they had done before the war. Now they knew more about what kind of land they wanted. They weren't looking for a normal acre or tract of land in a heavily trafficked neighborhood. Frank Lloyd Wright had told them to look for a piece of property that no one else wanted—the kind of property not yet discovered, not yet leveled by any developers. This piece of property should have interesting features, perhaps a natural sloping of the land, trees, a sense of nature.

One real estate agent showed them land off Lincoln Road and near Telegraph Road in the Birmingham area. Then he showed them two more pieces of property nearby: an acre of land in a very wooded area and, across the road, two rather barren acres. Sara thought that the two acres, which had no trees, looked absolutely desolate. She didn't like the fact that the wooded acre—the one Smithy liked the best—was across the street from such a forlorn place. Nor did she like the idea of being near such a busy thoroughfare as Telegraph Road. In fact, she had a distaste for the whole area. But Smithy and the agent talked, and Smithy, excited about finding his wooded acre, wrote out a check for $500 and gave it to the agent as a deposit.

"I did not feel at peace about the whole thing," Sara says, "but I had the philosophy that we don't always know where our blessings lie, and if the land was to be a blessing to all concerned, then we would get the green light on it. If it was not right, something would block it, so I just left it in God's hands. But Smithy was so enthusiastic! While we were driving home, he kept repeating how wonderful this land was. How could I dampen that enthusiasm? So I said, 'Yes, dear, it is.' What a happy husband I had! And that was worth everything to me."

A couple of days after Smithy and Sara had paid their deposit on the land, the telephone rang. When Sara answered, a man at the other end of the phone asked, "Does a Melvyn Maxwell Smith live at this address?"

"Yes, he does."

"Does he have a brother-in-law named Irving Goldberg?"

"Yes, that's correct."

"Thank you."

The caller hung up, and Sara thought, "How queer!" Three days later, Smithy's check was returned with a note advising that the owner had decided not to sell the property.

"Not being able to buy that property was the answer to my prayer," says Sara. "But when Smithy got home and I showed him the letter, he was upset. We would have to start looking all over again."

It wasn't any stretch of the imagination to put that phone call and the returned check together and to realize their check had been returned because they were Jewish. In those days, people made no secret of refusing to sell real estate to Jews or Blacks. It didn't matter if the prospective buyers had fought for their country during the war, if they were teaching in the school system, if they paid taxes, paid their bills on time and were model citizens. Schools, restaurants, movie theaters and lunchrooms were off limits for Blacks in many parts of the country, and signs declaring "Whites Only" or "No Negroes Allowed" were openly tolerated throughout America. Social clubs, country clubs, professional societies, private swimming pools and college fraternities and sororities openly, and self-righteously, excluded Jews, Blacks and other minorities on a regular basis.

Many legal contracts also bound homeowners *not* to sell to Jews or Blacks at any later time. This too was legal, an open policy. But sometimes, real estate agents would avoid conflict by saying politely that the land wasn't available or otherwise sidestep the actual practices and policies. The agent's response to the Smiths—*the property in question is no longer for sale*—is a code still practiced on occasion to get around anti-discrimination laws that now make such behavior illegal.

And while Sara wasn't unhappy about losing that land, she did feel sorry for Smithy. Besides being angry, he was despondent about not having a piece of property for his Frank Lloyd Wright house. And further searching was proving fruitless. "I realized I had to do a lot of praying and listening," says Sara. "So one afternoon, I got the idea to pick up the yellow pages that listed the names of developers. I called several, but none of them helped. Then I looked for realtors out in the northern suburban area, the west part of Detroit and the east part. I talked to those realtors and they said that land in those areas would be sudivided in the very near future, maybe within two or three years.

"I kept looking in the yellow pages, and then my eye was led to the name of a real estate company in the Birmingham area by the name of James, Walsh and Wacey. As it happened, it was one of the most prestigious realtors in the area at the time. So I called them up and asked for Mr. James. When I talked to him, I told him that my husband and I were both Jewish, and then I told him how hard we had been trying to find real estate in the area and the story of how our check had been returned. He was very kind, and somehow we got talking about our philosophies of life, and our values and the importance of just living and loving our fellow man. For more than a half an hour, we had a charming conversation. At the end of it, he said, 'You know, the stipulations that we make in our contracts isn't to keep away people like you. We want people like you to live out here.' He said, 'I would love to meet you and your husband, and if you'd like, I will show you some of our choice pieces of property.'"

Sara set up an appointment for Smithy to meet with Mr. James, and when Smithy came home and heard about it, he was relieved. He was even happier once he had met Mr. James and re-established the search. One day, after looking at properties in Bloomfield Hills, Smithy came home exhilarated. He told Sara that the undeveloped land with its woods and marshes was beautiful and wild, just the kind of property that would be perfect for a home designed by Frank Lloyd Wright. At one point, Smithy reported, he and Mr. James had been driving through the Lone Pine Estates, when they turned on to Pon Valley Road. Going up a hill, Smithy noticed a spot that was rather rugged and overgrown with greenery and trees. He said, "Please stop. That spot looks very interesting." As Mr. James backed down the hill, Smithy looked at how the land sloped down toward a wet marshy area with a small pond. Wright had suggested a piece of hilly property, and something about this landscape struck Smithy's imagination. He asked, "Is this place for sale?"

Mr. James searched on his chart of properties and finally said, "Yes, it is."

"What's the price?"

"Four thousand seven hundred dollars. That's for three and a third acres."

Smithy knew that he and Sara could only pay $3,600—and that would mean using every nickel of their savings, which was $2,000 from Smithy's Army days and $1,600 from Sara's salary. Nevertheless, he loved that piece of land. "I'm going to go home and get my wife and bring her out here," he said. "If she likes this piece of property as much as I do, we'll put in our bid."

When Smithy drove Sara and two-year-old Bobby out to see the property, Sara also fell in love with it. "I felt such peace and serenity there," she says. "The land was a wilderness of trees, swamp and over-grown greenery, but it had a wonderful feeling about it. It reminded me of pictures I had seen in *Beauty and the Beast* of gnarled oak trees, marshland and wilderness. I was so thrilled. I knew this was the right place."

The property was just what Frank Lloyd Wright had told them to find: "something nobody wants in the middle of nowhere." When they got home, Smithy called Mr. James and told him they loved the property and wanted it, but they couldn't meet the price of $4,700. They just didn't have that much money. What they could offer was $3,600—and not a penny more. Was there any possibility that the owners would accept that amount?

Mr. James said that two sisters owned the property. He would call them and submit the Smiths' offer and see what happened.

Smithy was distraught. The difference between $3,600 and $4,700 was significant. The owners would never want to go that low. Sara, on the other hand, felt a relaxed confidence about their prospects. She told him, "You know, Smithy, if this is the place that God wants for us, nobody else can have it."

After a sleepless night, Sara and Smithy heard from Mr. James. Apparently the sisters owned hundreds of acres in the Lone Pine Estates area. They had inherited the land from their parents, and each year they sold off only a small portion of the land—just enough—to pay their property taxes. When their taxes were paid for the year, then they weren't interested in selling any more land until the following year. That year, 1946, it just happened that the sisters hadn't sold their quota of land before they'd received their tax bill. The previous week, the tax bill had arrived and they owed exactly $3,500 in property taxes. So, since $3,600 would cover their tax bill and give them $100 extra, they would agree to Smithy and Sara's offer. It was just exactly what they needed!

Smithy could hardly believe their good fortune, and Sara, though not at all surprised, was just as thrilled. "Finally we owned a piece of property in Bloomfield Hills that we both loved!" she says. "We were so excited about it. I brought my mother out to see the property, and she was very impressed with it, but she couldn't understand why we would want to move so far from the city. She said, 'Why in heaven's name are you going to move way out here in the wilderness?'

"In fact, most of our friends who knew about the property thought we were a bit crazy. It really did seem like a long way from the city, and because it was undeveloped, it seemed to them that we were moving out into the wilderness."

Sara's sisters and their families often went to the property with her in the spirit of a country outing. "We used to have to go out to the highway or out Woodward Avenue and then down Lone Pine in order to get here," remembers Thelma's son and Bobby's first cousin, Marvin Shwedel. "This was like a sanctuary, like the end of the world. My uncle's foresight was fantastic. This is the heart of Bloomfield Hills, which is the most exclusive suburb, really, of Detroit. And when he got this acreage, nearly the whole area was vacant. The Everell Fishers, of Fisher Body and General Motors, they owned all the land across the road from the Smith's property. There were a couple of other people out here, and that was about it. There were no paved roads, no expressways. So, when we came out here, it really was like going to the end of the world."

The deal was closed. And as soon as they could raise the money, Smithy hired surveyors and a draftsman to make a topographical study showing the geographical configurations of the property. He also took pictures of the land, as Wright had suggested. With topographical sketches and photographs in hand, he was ready to contact Frank Lloyd

Wright to tell him he'd found *the* property. On August 17, 1946, with
Labor Day rapidly approaching, Smithy sent a telegram to Wright at
Taliesin, Spring Green, Wisconsin:

REFERENCE PAGES 245 AND 246 IN YOUR WORK ON
ARCHITECTURE I HAVE THE HOMESITE MAY I COME IN
SOMETIME TO SEE YOU BETWEEN NOW AND THE END OF
THE MONTH TO DISCUSS PLANS FOR THE HOUSE THAT
WAS MEANT FOR THE SITE PLEASE WIRE AT 17089 VAN
BUREN DETROIT

One week passed, and then another. Finally Smithy got Frank
Lloyd Wright's response—"*Glad to see you any time—let us know when.
Frank Lloyd Wright.*" By that time, it seemed clear that Smithy would
have to take the sketches out to Taliesin over Labor Day weekend. The
prospect thrilled, but also upset Smithy, who hated to fly. Just the idea
of flying made him anxious because he was always afraid of a crash,
afraid *something* would happen. On the other hand, he would start
teaching on the Tuesday after Labor Day, and he couldn't get to Taliesin
and back in time if he drove. He knew that if he didn't go out to
Wisconsin over Labor Day, then he would have to wait many more
weeks—at least until Thanksgiving or Christmas vacation—to go. So, he
accepted the offer and made reservations to fly from Detroit to
Madison, Wisconsin, over Labor Day weekend.

When the weekend came, Smithy flew to Madison and then took a
bus to Spring Green. From Spring Green, he walked to Taliesin. The
day was dusty and hot, and by the time he arrived at Taliesin, he was
dirty, sweaty and exhausted. Nevertheless, Taliesin was a shady, breezy
place even on the hot summer afternoon, and after resting on a stone
bench in the shade and drinking some lemonade, he began to feel
refreshed. The architects who greeted him asked why he hadn't called.
"We would have been very happy to come and pick you up!" one said
to him. "We always pick people up!"

Feeling somewhat chagrined, Smithy was shown to his room, where
he showered, changed clothes and prepared for the evening. Weekends

at Taliesin in those days were filled with music, fascinating guests and dynamic conversations that took place inside in the distinctive, open rooms and outside within walled courts, on cantilevered terraces with stone seats, and around the hill garden bordered with flowers and limestone walls.

Afternoon tea was served in the tea circle, a half circle of wall within the garden that was a shady, comfortable place for visiting and relaxing even on hot summer days. The sound of running water in the pools and fountains added a sense of misty, cool gentility. Often on Saturdays, following afternoon tea, guests would sit down to a formal dinner and then go into the auditorium for a concert. Any guests who played instruments or sang were encouraged to participate. On these occasions, Frank Lloyd Wright would most often be dressed in a striking white linen suit, ascot and white shoes.

On that particular weekend, the guests at Taliesin included a well-known weaver from New York, Dorothy Lietest, and others of whom Smithy had heard. Smithy later told Sara that the well-known guests made him feel insignificant, but that didn't stop him from enjoying himself.

In truth, the atmosphere lifted Smithy into another realm of fantasy-become-reality and filled him with dreams of the kind of gatherings he and Sara might someday host themselves. "Just to be in that atmosphere, just to be in the school, just to walk into the drafting room was astounding," he told Sara later. "It was the greatest experience!"

On Sunday morning, Frank Lloyd Wright gave a stimulating talk to the whole school, the staff and the guests. But while Smithy was still enjoying the experience, he was beginning to feel anxious and concerned about his house plans. After all, it was Sunday and nothing had been mentioned about his home. He had given the topographical map to Wright when he arrived, but Wright hadn't said one word to him about it. In fact, beyond a polite nod in his direction and a hello, Wright hadn't said one word to him about *anything*. Smithy knew he would be leaving Monday afternoon, so just when would he get to talk to Frank Lloyd Wright about designing his house? Maybe he wouldn't get to talk to him at all. Everything seemed so programmed, so busy, and it was beginning to seem that he wasn't going to find out anything. What if he had to go home having accomplished nothing? It wasn't as if they had the money for him to fly out here again. If something didn't happen, they might have to wait another year or more before Mr. Wright would start the design.

By Monday morning, Smithy was quite agitated. He tried not to show it, but he was worried. After breakfast, however, he went with one of the younger architects into the drafting room, and there was Frank Lloyd Wright, with his apprentices gathered around him, looking at Smith's topographical map, which was spread across the drafting table. "Mr. Smith has given us a challenge," Wright said. "He's commissioned us to design a home for him on this land."

Smithy, greatly relieved, listened to the architects discussing the topography with Wright. He enjoyed the camaraderie that enveloped the discussion. But watching Wright look at and talk about the topographical map and the photographs was on par with witnessing a master painter coming to his easel, dipping his brush into the paint. Smithy knew that these maps and photos were mere guides for such a master; the design itself would come from his imagination and inspiration. "It was like watching a master conductor reading a score," Smithy would later say. "It was like listening to music."

Before he left Taliesin, Smithy couldn't resist asking Wright, "When do you think I can expect my plans?"

Frank Lloyd Wright looked at Smithy for a moment without comment. Then he said, without irony or sarcasm, "When the spirit moves me."

Smithy thanked him, but said to himself, "I certainly hope the spirit moves him fast."

*"Love is not passive," says Sara. "Love is reflected in actions—
a handshake, a smile, a kind word, a good deed."*

Chapter 12

THE DESIGN OF THEIR DREAMS

W HEN SMITHY RETURNED FROM TALIESIN, he and Sara vowed to be even more frugal so that they would be able to make the necessary payments for the design and building of their Frank Lloyd Wright home. Sara's salary could help significantly. So, Sara, who hadn't taught since Bobby was born, went to the Board of Education and landed a job at the Longfellow School, once again teaching "auditorium."

On the first Tuesday of September, both Sara and Smithy got up early to get dressed for the first day of school. Sara was extremely upset because it was the first time she had ever left Bobby, who was two years old. He would be spending the day with a neighbor.

"She was a very nice woman, lovely and very efficient," says Sara. "She was a nurse, and we were so fortunate to find someone like her. She would be taking care of Bobby and three other children in her own nearby apartment. When we left for school, she was holding Bobby in her arms and Bobby was waving to us, not a tear in his eyes. It was the first time, really, that I had ever left him, so there was no such thing as 'Don't go, Mommy!' He just waved his hand and looked a little bewildered. We drove off and I burst into tears. Smithy said, 'I'm not worried about Bobby. I'm more concerned about you.'

"Well, I straightened up and Smithy drove me to the Longfellow School, and I began teaching again." As usual, Sara brought an unusual exuberance to her teaching, and even though she didn't like being away from her son, once again, she was tremendously successful. (In later years, she would combine her roles as mother and teacher when Bobby was a student in her third grade auditorium class.)

On weekends, Smithy, Sara and Bobby didn't go out to eat unless it was at the home of friends or family—usually at Thelma's or at Jennie's. Nor did they go to movies. They had fun, but they saved in small ways as well as large ones. For instance, they never ordered a newspaper or had one delivered because they could both read the paper at school for free, which at the time meant they saved about two dollars a month. They took their trash in bags and dropped it off at school or at Thelma's house, a bag at a time, so they wouldn't have to pay the trash company the monthly pick-up bill. Nor did they spend money on clothes. Sara had plenty of clothes from earlier days, and she rotated them so that the children she taught wouldn't get tired of seeing her in the same outfits or colors every day. She used different scarves and belts to change and dress things up, and she always looked chic. Smithy, also quite a dapper figure, got his sports coats and pants, as well as casual clothes, from his brother Marty, an oral surgeon, who was the same size as he was. He never bought a suit—not even later, when he was could afford to buy one.

Every day when Sara and Smithy got home from school, they looked in the mail for the house plans to arrive from Wisconsin. Day after day, week after week, the mailbox only held letters and bills. They kept telling each other, "When the spirit moves him, we'll get the plans!"

In the meantime, after their first year at Herman Gardens, the Smiths had moved to a duplex apartment—a "Practical Homebuilders' Apartment"—on Elmhurst near Livernois, quite close to the Long-fellow School. One Sunday afternoon when Smithy was out taking a walk with Bobby near Elmhurst Avenue, he bumped into an old friend of his named Larry Kunin, who was walking with his daughter, Shirley, a child about Bobby's age. Larry and Smithy had gone to high school together, had belonged to the same Boy Scout troop, and liked each other enormously. Now they discovered that they lived in the same area. Smithy, exuberant at the serendipitous meeting, insisted Larry and Shirley come home with him to meet Sara. Later that same day, Larry brought his wife Esther over to meet Sara and the two hit it off, so much so that the two families began to spend a great deal of time together.

Meanwhile, 1946 came to an end. But still, the Smiths hadn't heard from Frank Lloyd Wright or seen any plans. They had never received the letter that Frank Lloyd Wright's secretary Eugene Masselink had sent to them care of Gregor Affleck, another client of Wright's, in Bloomfield Hills on November 14, 1946. That letter stated:

Dear Mr. Smith:
The preliminary drawings for your house will be ready in a few
days. Kindly let me know where we should send them.

Unaware of any communication from Wright, Smithy sent a Western Union telegram, today's equivalent of express mail, on January 20, 1947:

FRANK LLOYD WRIGHT:
MAKING INQUIRY AS TO PROGRESS OF PRELIMINARY
PLANS FOR MY HOME ABOUT WHICH WE HAD DISCUSSED
AT TALIESIN ON MY VISIT SEPTEMBER 1, 1946. HAVE
BEEN LOOKING FORWARD EAGERLY FOR SKETCHES.
WOULD APPRECIATE HEARING FROM YOU.

A few days later, Smithy received a response from Eugene Masselink saying that the drawings were ready and would be sent on very soon. But, no sketches came. On February 28, Smithy wrote again, and in early March, Eugene Masselink wrote again for Frank Lloyd Wright, explaining that the package containing the preliminary studies for the house had somehow been lost in the mail. They were tracing the package, and if it wasn't found, they would send another set.

One Sunday afternoon about a week later, Smithy and Sara invited Larry and Esther Kunin to drive with them out Woodward Avenue to take a look at a house designed by Frank Lloyd Wright for Gregor and Betty Affleck. The Affleck house, which Wright had designed in 1940, had been the first Wright home in the area. Smithy had heard it was quite extraordinary both inside and out, and although he'd driven by the house before, he wanted to look at it again and show it to his friends. What Smithy and Sara didn't know at the time was that Gregor Affleck had been a childhood friend of Wright's. The two had grown up together, and so Wright felt a particularly special attachment both to the Afflecks and their home, where he stayed whenever he was in Detroit for business or a lecture.

The afternoon was sunny and clear when the two families drove out Woodward Avenue and parked outside the Affleck home in Bloomfield Hills. From their car, they couldn't see the house well. It sat on a sloping ravine and was somewhat hidden by lush foliage and trees, so they decided to get out for a better view. Smithy had just stepped out of the car when a man walked toward them. He walked right over to Smithy, held out his hand, and introduced himself as Gregor Affleck, owner of the house. When Smithy introduced himself, Affleck looked shocked, and then an enormous smile spread across his face as he repeated, "Melvyn Maxwell Smith?

"Are you really Melvyn Maxwell Smith?" he asked.

"I am," Smithy said, confused.

"I can't believe it!" Affleck said. "Taliesin seems to have lost your address, so they sent your house plans to me in the hopes that I could locate you. I tried hard, but I wasn't successful. *You* try to find a Smith in Detroit when you have no idea where he lives!"

"Do you mean you have our plans?"

"No, I sent them back to Taliesin. But if you contact Mr. Wright, I'm sure you'll get them to you very shortly."

Smithy was stunned, but when Gregor Affleck invited them all in for a tour of the house, he tried to control his excitement. Certainly a tour of the house was more than they'd imagined. Sara later said that as she walked through Gregor and Betty Affleck's home and looked through the glass windows to the trees, she was absolutely astounded. Besides Taliesin, which was so big, this was the first Frank Lloyd Wright home she had ever been inside, and the lighting was extraordinary. Both she and Smithy were intoxicated by the beauty of the house, by its simplicity and grandeur. The Afflecks' impeccable artistic taste complimented the gorgeous 16-foot-tall cypress walls in the living room that were canted, not vertical. The Afflecks had lush plants indoors and outdoors, and water lilies floating in a small reflective pond were mirrored in the windows of a glass atrium. A balcony off the living area hung over a bluff, creating, almost literally, a bird's eye view of nature.

When Smithy and Sara got home after dropping off the Kunins at their house, Smithy went straight to the telephone to call Taliesin. All his reserve, all of the holding back of his anxiety had been released with Afflecks' news that the plans were, in fact, completed. Affleck had held them in his hands, and no doubt, now Smithy and Sara would soon see those plans themselves. The spirit had moved Frank Lloyd Wright and their house had been designed! That fact was a tangible reality.

On March 24, Eugene Masselink wrote that the drawings were being sent via registered airmail. A few days later, the package containing the preliminary studies for the house, the general plans, and the drawings of the elevations arrived. With shaking hands, Smithy opened the package and laid the studies out on the kitchen table. *The Melvyn Maxwell Smith House*, the name printed in the bottom corner of the paper, was no longer just a crazy dream.

The elongated, single-floor plan was laid out on a two-foot by four-foot grid, looking something like an upside-down T. This house was a classic example of what Wright called the Usonian house—a design that would integrate the beauty of the indoors and outdoors *and* be within the affordable reach of ordinary people. At the same time, it was a house tailored to the individual's needs. Wright had designed his first Usonian home in response to the challenge from a journalist named Herbert Jacobs in Madison, Wisconsin. Wright had done it so masterfully that it became a model for many other Usonian houses that followed. The Jacobs' house in Madison, the one Smithy had referred to when he first spoke to Frank Lloyd Wright, was built in the shape of an L, with a central kitchen work area and abundant natural light provided by banks of floor-to-ceiling windows oriented to the back of the house, with minimal windows facing the road at the front.

Like the Jacobs' House, the Smith house also was designed with what Wright called "zones" for living. In the living zone were the living and dining areas—configured not as separate rooms, but rather open spaces that flowed into each other. There were two family bedrooms and a guest bedroom in the sleeping zone. And the utility zone contained the kitchen in the core part of the house, pivotal to the living zone. The house had sleek, distinctly Japanese lines, and like the Jacobs' and other Usonian homes, it did not have a "street presence" with decorative features in the front. Indeed, from the front, the house looked low-slung and simple, ornamented only with small functional windows around the top to let in light. In the back, however, glorious floor-to-ceiling windows opened to the gently sloping hill, the marshes, the pond, the trees and the rest of nature's garden. This was in keeping with Wright's sense of organic architecture, relating the building to the site of the natural landscape, where the interior and the exterior are unified. In the Smiths' case, Wright had it planned so that the house would tuck into a hillock of the landscape.

Instead of having a garage, the house would have a carport, and instead of pitched-roof, the house would have a wide and flat over-hanging roof made from a simple, insulated slab that contained a ven-tilation system. Wright had no use for basements, and so the house would be built on another slab, equipped with a new kind of central heating—a hot-water radiant system. This system was produced by hot water pipes embedded in a drained bed of sand and cinders under the concrete slab floors. The circulation of hot water below the floors would warm the entire house, and light coming in at certain angles through the windows during the winter would add solar heat.

Wright designed what were essentially prefabricated walls using three layers of board and two of tar paper, wanting the house to be built with every possible labor- and money-saving shortcut. Other pages of the plan showed how the house would be finished inside with a board and batten wall system of cypress panels screwed together. While the plan was cost-effective, it retained all of the essential attributes of a Frank Lloyd Wright design—the sense of spatial surprise when walking in from relative darkness to an abundance of light, with meticulous attention to aesthetic details and the use of natural light. A changing mural of nature would be provided by the floor-to-ceiling windows that ran across the back and wrapped around corners of the house.

For Sara, the plans were exciting, and she looked on with curiosity and interest as Smithy explained the layout and the concepts of a Usonian home. For Smithy, however, the plans were more than fasci-nating and exciting; they were the dream he had been carrying inside of him for years. The papers he held in his hands were key to elevating the meaning of his existence. Smithy sat riveted hour after hour, studying the details, thinking, smiling, frowning, jotting down notes to himself.

In April, Smithy received another letter from Frank Lloyd Wright's secretary at Taliesin West:

> *Dear Mr. Smith:*
> *The drawings for your house were mailed to you on March 26th and we trust you received them safely. We have never been able to unravel the mystery of what became of them after they were sent to us from Taliesen, but I believe they must have been misaddressed. We are extremely sorry for the delay involved.*

Smithy wrote back a long handwritten letter that began:

> *Dear Mr. Wright,*
> *The preliminary studies for our house infinitely please us. We appreciate with much regard the general plan of house and lot, which appears to be most suitable for the site. The proposed cost of twenty thousand dollars also is acceptable should it not range beyond that. Your conception has helped us to realize more vividly the house we want to call 'My Haven.'*

Smithy asked several questions and enclosed a check for six hundred dollars, the first three percent of Wright's architectural fee.

In early May, 1947, Frank Lloyd Wright wrote:

> *Dear Mr. and Mrs. Smith:*
> *Thank you. We are glad you like the house. In order to proceed with the working drawings we shall need the preliminary sketches. When you are ready kindly mail them to us at Spring Green. We shall be there after the 15th of May. All of your suggestions shall have careful attention.*
> *Sincerely yours,*
> *Frank Lloyd Wright, Taliesin West, Scottsdale, Arizona.*

Smithy returned the preliminary sketches, and once again, a long wait was in store. In mid-July, Masselink wrote that the plans and specifications would be ready in about three weeks, and in mid-September, he wrote again to say that the plans had been delayed, and while they hoped to send them as soon as possible, they hesitated to make any promises. Smithy sent wires in October and November and again in December. On December 11, Frank Lloyd Wright wired back:

> *Just getting settled at Taliesin West. Sorry for continued delay. Work on your plans nearing completion. Best wishes. Frank Lloyd Wright.*

On January 24, Frank Lloyd Wright wrote Smithy that three sets of prints of the working drawings for the house had been mailed directly from the blueprinting company in Phoenix. Smithy, ecstatic, sent a thousand dollars to Wright with the notation, "5% of $20,000 proposed cost as according to schedule herewith." In a letter to Wright he said he would submit the working plans to various trade contractors for bids and let Wright know their proposed construction costs and whether it would be feasible to begin construction within the year.

Wright wrote back:

> *As conditions are now there is little point in turning your plans over to the trade contractors. They do not know the construction but figure cubic or floor area prices. In order to keep costs in line we shall have to quantity survey for you and budget separate bids locally, as according to the outline in the schedule of architect's services sent you. Faithfully, Frank Lloyd Wright.*

That spring, with the working plans in hand, Smithy again spent hours at the kitchen table or at his desk, studying details, making notes. Wright had made estimates of costs, but the estimates Smithy got from contractors and builders were three or four times more expensive. One night after working over the plans and sheets of figures, Smithy stood up with a desperately sad look on his face and said, "Sara, you and I cannot afford to build this home. We don't have the money for it. It's just impossible."

Their house was only 1800 square feet, half the size of the Afflecks, but it was clear that the Afflecks had money that the Smiths did not. Even a house this small would cost too much. By the time they paid for a contractor and builder, as well as the cost of labor and materials —especially all that cypress and glass and brick—the costs would be prohibitive. Affordable for someone else, perhaps, but simply too much for them. If Smithy had been a man prone to tears, he would have been crying. Sara, however, encouraged him to believe that if this house was part of God's plan for them, it would happen. They had to trust and believe that this home was a reality, and that somehow, someway, it would work out. They read Sara's prayer about home together and once again, Smithy became hopeful.

Almost every night after he finished teaching and grading papers, and after he, Sara and Bobby had dinner in their cozy little apartment, Smithy would sit, pouring over Wright's plans and making his calculations for their new home. "I remember my dad when I was three, four and five years old," says Bob. "This was when we owned the property, but he hadn't built the house because he didn't have enough money. After dinner, he would go into his room, and he would look at those plans hour after hour after hour, night after night. The plans were maybe ten or twelve pages altogether—I've forgotten how many —but every night, he would be there. And I remember him looking at a page, flipping it over, looking at it again. I always wondered, what did he see there? But I didn't understand at that time—he was already imagining it built. He was already building it in his own mind. He looked at that plan, and it was like he was in the house. But I didn't understand that then. I'd say, 'Daddy, you've already seen the plans.' But Mom was as supportive as anyone could be. She never argued —never."

During those nightly sessions with the plans, Smithy memorized every nook and cranny of his dream house. And he and Sara and Bobby often took picnics and visited their land—going for walks, playing catch or just sitting, imagining how someday they would live there. In the meantime, they were saving their money for the day they would actually begin to build.

Overall, Smithy was thrilled with the design; he loved it and thought it was nearly perfect. But during his months of concentration on the plans, he had started identifying a few small faults—elements that he thought should be changed. He wasn't entirely conscious of the fact that no one made changes on Frank Lloyd Wright's plans or that Wright's wrath was legendary. He hadn't heard that Wright often said, "People come to me and tell me what they want, and I tell them what they need." In this case, Smithy had specific design details he thought *needed* to be changed. The main problem, as Smithy saw it, was that the clerestory windows—the small windows that ran above the side and front walls of the living room—terminated at the core of the house. Why did they stop there? Why didn't they go all the way around that part of the house?

Smithy wanted to put the house plans into action. Finally, in July, he wrote Frank Lloyd Wright to ask if he and Sara could visit Taliesin sometime between August 8 to 30th to discuss certain features of the house and make arrangements for future construction.

Frank Lloyd Wright wrote back that they were welcome anytime.

So, in August of 1949, Sara and Smithy left Bobby with Betty Gold, Smithy's sister, and her family, and set out for Spring Green, Wisconsin. Smithy felt so confident about the changes he wanted in the design that it never occurred to him not to suggest them. This time, when they drove up to Taliesin, they felt they were returning to a familiar, beloved place. And, as clients of Frank Lloyd Wright's, they were treated with utmost courtesy and regard.

When it was time to meet with Wright, Sara and Smithy both went to the drafting studio, where Smithy sat to the left of Frank Lloyd Wright and Sara sat to his right. Feeling suddenly anxious about his intentions, Smithy said, "Before you open the plans, I want you to know that in studying them, I made some changes. You don't need to look at them if you don't want to. And of course, if you disapprove, we'll just forget about the changes I made."

Frank Lloyd Wright didn't respond to Smithy or answer him in any way. He began to look through the plans, and while he did so, he focused on Smithy's changes—the most dramatic being Smithy's suggestion that the upper level clerestory windows not stop before they get to the utility core, as Wright had designated. Instead, the windows would continue all the way around and through the utility core, which would add natural light from the west to the kitchen and the library, the small room next to the kitchen. Smithy had suggested on one of the blueprints that the interior brick core, which ascended 12 or 13 feet into the interior ceiling height, could be lowered partially in some areas, especially in the small library and the utility room, to accommodate the change. Then the clerestory windows could continue on around to meet the upper level of the bedroom units that butted up to the brick core on the east side of the house. Without these upper level windows, it seemed, the kitchen would be too dark. Smithy could find no logical reasons for the windows to stop so soon. And besides, this change would conform to Wright's concept of continuity and unity in that it would carry the clerestory windows around the entire brick side of the house.

Wright took his time on Smithy's suggested alterations in the design. Finally he stood up, turned and tapped his pencil on the drafting table. He tapped and tapped, seemingly lost in thought. Then he looked at Sara and said, "Your husband would have made a fine architect." He not only agreed with Smithy's changes, but he said they were an improvement. At that moment, Smithy later said, he felt as if he had been awarded his degree in architecture.

Wright then called in Jack Howe to get the plans, and said, "Jack, I want you to make the corrections in these plans that Smith has suggested." Jack Howe looked at Wright a little quizzically and then picked up the plans. Detroit architectural writer Dale Northrup would later say that it probably was one of the few times that the client collaborated so closely with Frank Lloyd Wright on the design of the house.

The relationship between Smith and Wright was so remarkable that much later, Wesley Peters, Frank Lloyd Wright's chief draftsman (and future president of the Frank Lloyd Wright Foundation) would say,

"You need two things to produce a great building—a great architect and a great client. Smith was a great client. All of Wright's great architectural pieces, his great buildings, are the result of that kind of relationship between the client and the architect.

"Frank Lloyd Wright had many wonderful client relationships. He had wealthier clients, and he had ones with much bigger estates or buildings, who had wider opportunities. But he never had clients who were greater in the sense of love and appreciation than Melvyn Maxwell and Sara Smith. It was a two-way road because the more that came back to Frank Lloyd Wright, the more he gave, so it was a double gain.

"He had all of Smith's changes incorporated into his developed preliminary drawings because he appreciated Smith's input. This was the kind of relationship that continued with them constantly through the building and construction and after the construction of this house. Smith executed Wright's design to perfection, and it is still one of the best maintained homes in the country."

The meeting of Wright and Smith's minds over those house plans was something that Sara would never forget. "What a great man Mr. Wright was," she says. "I admired and respected him so much. You know you would hear about all of his arrogance, but he really expressed such humility, and he was such a kind and spiritual person."

After staying for a few days and feeling very satisfied with their interview with Wright, Sara and Smithy went back to Detroit, picked up Bobby and returned to their respective schools. In early September, they received a revised sheet of house drawings that incorporated all of Smithy's suggested changes. They were on their way.

ABOVE: Bobby helps to move sand that was used to mix cement during the building of their home in 1949. BELOW: Sara hoses debris away from the foundation.

ABOVE: Bobby plays as the bricklayer starts to build an interior wall of the house. BELOW: Smithy and Bobby cool off in July, 1950, two months after moving into their new home.

ABOVE AND BELOW: The house in the late 1950s before the grounds were land-scaped.

Looking from the edge of the living room toward the south end of the house, where the original master bedroom was located.

Smithy looks over Frank Lloyd Wright's shoulder, during Wright's first visit to
the house in 1953.

Smithy talks with Frank Lloyd Wright and his wife, Olgivanna, on Wright's second visit to *My Haven* in the late 1950s.

Sara with Frank Lloyd Wright at his birthday celebration at Taliesin, in Spring Green, Wisconsin.

Sara and Smithy in the living room of their home.

"The only career there is," says Sara,
"is the career of love."

Chapter 13

SMITHY'S DREAMS BECOME
REALITY

FRANK LLOYD WRIGHT HAD TOLD SMITHY to call him when he was ready to start the job.

And, he gave Smithy advice that set him on a quicker path towards building. In desperation, Smithy had confessed to Wright that he was afraid that he and Sara could not actually afford to build the house, that they simply did not have the money. But Wright had contradicted and challenged him. "Of course you can afford to build this home," Wright said. "You don't have to pay a general contractor. You can be the general contractor."

Later Smithy would say, "Mr. Wright advised that I should build the house myself. He didn't mean that I should take hammer in one hand and saw in the other and get to work, although some of his clients have done just that. He explained that if I would study the plans until I was assured that I could supervise the building of it, then I should become its general contractor.

"As a general contractor, I would hire the various independent journeymen and laborers who would be attracted to work upon a Frank Lloyd Wright project for minimal compensation. Also as general contractor, I would be able to buy building materials at considerable discounts."

All through the fall months, Smithy studied the plans, saved and calculated in preparation for his job as supervisor. In late February, he wrote to Taliesen West:

Dear Mr. Wright,

*Our plans to construct our house in the late spring of this year
have been actively pursued. We have been awarded a building
permit and subdivision approval. We have found a young (but
experienced) and enthusiastic contractor who is willing to tackle
the project for the cost of labor and materials (as discounted to
contractor) plus a very modest fee. We have also arranged for
necessary millwork to be fabricated. . . .*

*May we order additional complete sets of blueprints from the
original tracings which you have? Subdivision association
wants one. Townships building department demands another
and others will be needed by contractor. We will be happy to pay
extra costs.*

*Sara and I are planning to welcome your apprentice as
early in May as you find it convenient to send him. . . .*

Sincerely yours,

Sara and Maxwell Smith.

The house plans were always spread out in front of Smithy or close
at hand. Smithy's friend Larry Kunin spent a lot of time with him, looking at the plans and talking about the materials Smithy would have to
purchase. Bricks, glass and red tidewater cypress were the materials
Smithy would need in the largest quantities. The cypress was not only
hard to get, but also quite expensive. Larry Kunin, however, wanted to
help, and since he was in the sweeping compound business, he had good
connections with lumberyards. When Larry and Smithy had run into
each other on the street with Bobby and Shirley, neither, of course, had
had any idea what a large role Larry would end up playing in the building of Smithy and Sara's house. But as the plans to build progressed,
Larry stepped in with an expertise that astounded Smithy.

To start, Kunin called suppliers and succeeded in ordering red tidewater cypress at a much lower-than-normal price. (Altogether, Smithy
eventually was able to purchase over 14,000 board feet of the redwater
cypress and have it milled for less than one-third of his early estimates.)

And when Smithy bemoaned the fact that he probably never would be able to find a crew willing to work for minimum wage, Larry said, "Wrong! I think I have just the man for you! And he has a friend he works with. They're a great team." The two young builders, Peter Turczyn and Steve Kovacs, got excited about the house plans and agreed to work for two dollars an hour after their regular jobs. Peter Turczyn's brother happened to be an electrician, and both Peter and Steve had other friends and relatives in the trades who were interested in moonlighting on a Frank Lloyd Wright house. With those two at its center, Smithy had his crew. He also had a lot of his supplies. After school hours, Smithy had been roaming brickyards until he found a yard with the lowest prices on common brick and purchased all the bricks he would need. With Kunin's help, he also found an inexpensive source of crushed rock and sand, as well as plywood and other materials.

Frank Lloyd Wright wrote that he would be in the Kalamazoo area about May 25th and would see Smithy and Sara at that time to discuss further construction details and the journeyman apprentice who would be assigned to the job. Smithy wrote back saying that the contractor was ready to begin excavating on May 15th and didn't want to delay because he felt that any delay would prevent his getting the desired help he had hired for the project. Smithy hoped that the journeyman apprentice could arrive shortly before May 15th for the early phases of construction to permit the contractor to start work at a more suitable time for him.

On May 16th, Smithy wrote to Frank Lloyd Wright that they had begun the preliminary preparation of the site and were ready to proceed with construction. Each morning, Smithy, Sara and Bobby went to their schools. But when the school day ended and Smithy had driven Sara and Bobby home, he would grab a bite and go right out to Pon Valley Road. There he would meet up with Peter Turczyn and Steve Kovacs, who had worked at their regular building jobs during the day and arrived at the site ready to work until midnight.

The first thing the Smith-Turczyn-Kovacs team did was stake out the house to establish its proper placement on the property. Then they excavated 42-inch-deep trenches for the dry-well footings around the perimeter of the house—which would have a floating slab construction. When they began the digging, they discovered that the soil was consistently sandy, which was great, because water drains easily in sandy soil. (Clay soil holds the water and doesn't drain easily.)

The weather in May seemed to be in favor of the project, and everyone was taking great pride in their work, which was thorough and accurate. Step by step, Smithy was checking everything. Frank Lloyd Wright's trip to Kalamazoo had been delayed, and on June 1st, Smithy wrote to Wright, asking him a number of questions about substitute materials, and adding:

> *The housesite has been graded and leveled, the contour of house started, the foundations dug, drain tile placed, and the crushed rock fill poured. We are getting ready to pour the shallow concrete footings. Rough plumbing and placing electrical conduit is to follow soon. We're moving right along, Mr. Wright, and have experienced no difficulty as yet with the construction . . .*

During the summer, work on the house swung into a full-time occupation. Smithy reported to the property early in the morning and stayed until late at night. He pitched in where he could, picking up and hauling materials. He also frequently checked the plans, took measurements, watched and always supervised. Sometimes Sara and Bobby would go with him, have picnics on the grounds, and help with small tasks and picking up. Turczyn and Kovacs' relatives and friends also were coming to work on the house for minimum wage, usually after they had finished their other jobs—and often during the summer months, they would be there until 1:00 or 2:00 a.m.

When the men had dug down about a foot and removed all organic matter, they leveled, packed and re-packed the dirt for the foundation of the house. Then crushed rock and sand were poured into the whole excavated area, and a top layer of small aggregate rock was added. On top of aggregate rock, carefully planned lines of two-and-a-half-inch copper pipes were laid out in a snake-like fashion. These pipes, connected to a hot water heater, eventually would circulate hot water for the central heating system and provide gravity heat—usually referred to as radiant heat—for the entire house. During the winters, this heat would warm the concrete slab floors as well as the rooms, and during the summer, the floors would be cool.

Once the copper pipe was laid, it was time to put in the concrete slab floors—a complicated venture since it was so important that this process create a crack-free floor. They poured rough cement on top of the crushed rock, sand and copper piping in two-foot by four-foot mats. And then, on top of the leveled concrete, they poured a finish cement. This cement was mixed with a brick-colored powder that gave it a deep-red hue. "It was a beautiful color," remembers Sara, who watched the process. "It was fascinating to watch the men work. They were so exacting in everything they did."

With Smithy supervising, Turczyn and Kovacs and the other workers trawled the floor and scored it with two-foot by four-foot indentations. The scoring gave the floor a beautiful design that looked in many ways like large red tiles, but the scoring also had another purpose. Should there be cracks of any kind, they would show up at the scoring, which allowed for the expanding and contracting of the concrete. Once the floors were finished, they would contain the radiant heat from the pipes—a wonderful feature for bare feet in the winter. The floors also would look as if they were made of burnished leather.

"I remember when they laid those lines," says Bobby. "They had to site those lines to make sure that everything on the living room floor was perfect. Dad would come out and check everything, and every once in a while, he would say, 'Re-do this—re-do that.' One day I was real impressed with my dad because we were out there when a rattlesnake slithered across the floor. The concrete floor had been poured, and the rattlesnake was headed toward it. But my dad picked up two bricks, walked over to the rattlesnake, and caught its head in between the two bricks. Then he held up the rattlesnake, carried it away from the floor, dropped it, and then took a shovel out and blam-slam !*!# knocked its head off.

"I thought, 'Boy, is my dad brave.' But you know, he was thinking,

'That goddamn rattlesnake isn't going to screw up my floor!' He loved that floor. He loved everything about the house, and he was so happy driving up to watch it being built."

That summer Larry Kunin also helped Smithy find a fine cabinet maker—George Woods—who signed on for the project for three dollars an hour and began coming every day to work at the site. Smithy's brother-in-law, Irving Goldberg, who was Jennie's husband, also turned out to be an enormous help in the construction of the Smith house. Irving was quite successful in the cabinet manufacturing business and had installed cabinets and showcases for some of the finest stores in the area. He made arrangements for his business to cut to size all the cypress that would be used in the house, without charge. And through Irving, Smithy and Sara also were able to buy screws and hardware, such as the piano hinges that would be used on every door in the house, and any other building supplies they needed for less than cost.

Over the summer, the house began to go up, all of it ultimately discounted in materials and labor by thousands and thousands of dollars. One day, however, Smithy arrived to find that Kovacs and Turczyn and a journeyman mason hired to work with them had just completed laying the chimney. The men were exhausted, but the chimney was beautifully constructed and they were very proud of it. But when Smithy inspected it, he noticed that the placement of the bricks was one inch off. Almost anybody, knowing the costs involved, would have said fine, just keep building. There was not a structural problem, not a big deal in that sense. It was just a design glitch.

Smithy, however, said, "Boys, you've got to tear the chimney down." The men, shocked and offended by his reaction, said there was no way on earth that they were going to tear the chimney down. It was a perfectly built. What was one inch? It seemed clear that they would rather quit than destroy that brick chimney. But Smithy was firm. The bricks were perfectly aligned, but they were "off" by one inch, he told them, and that one inch could and would damage the integrity of the design of the rest of the house. "You've got to understand it from an artistic point of view," he said. "This place is living art, and it's got to be right."

So the chimney had to come down and be rebuilt—from the beginning—to specification. The men finally agreed to rebuild it *exactly* where it was supposed to go.

In mid-August, Frank Lloyd Wright's colleague and former apprentice, architect John Howe, wrote to Frank Lloyd Wright:

Dear Mr. Wright:

Herewith a report on the Melvyn Maxwell Smith house: All in all I found the work well advanced and well done. The house fits the site perfectly and will be more thrilling than the Rosenbaum house (a favorite of mine). It is a beautiful site, the house nestling down in sunlight with a view through beautiful trees to a cattail-filled pond beyond; all very intimate.

Though Mr. Smith is his own builder and does well, all things considered, the house is being built by a young contractor whose spirit and interest cannot be beat; he and his helper worked right through evenings and Sundays while I was there.

Mr. Smith is apt to be somewhat inch-wise and foot-foolish, overlooking general requirements in the face of particular complications, and tends to conduct the project as the school teacher which he is: questions and answers, every 'i' dotted and every point driven into the ground. I never worked so hard in my life. But they are good clients and have good understanding of the house. The brickwork is mostly up and is well done. I was dismayed, however, to find that the brick joint had not been preserved at either floor or ceiling, but won't show in most cases.

We framed the carport and lower room level while I was there. I was there two weeks and promised to return in three weeks when they would next most urgently need me. I made drawings for further cabinetwork and furniture details; these I will send for your approval.

During construction, many people walked around the grounds and through the house, especially on the weekends. "Great hoards of people who were interested in Frank Lloyd Wright's architecture would visit, and it was always amusing listening to them trying to figure out which room was a bedroom and what room was the kitchen," Sara remembers. "Invariably, they would get it all wrong. But Smithy was very generous about having people walk through, even when it when it was a crowd. He was always very cordial to anyone who stepped into this home."

The work progressed. Turczyn and Kovacs put up walls with three-quarter-inch plywood and then screwed cypress boards to it. Nothing was nailed; everything was joined together with brass screws that ran in four widely-spaced horizontal lines up the walls. Smithy was a perfectionist, which made him a tough taskmaster. Every screw was in perfect horizontal alignment.

But while the house was going up as planned, Smithy and Sara were beginning to run out of their savings as well as their current income. Since they'd gotten married, they'd been saving for their house, and since their return from the war, they had been setting aside all of Sara's salary and living as cheaply as they could on Smithy's. They'd built up a good-sized account, but building the house was rapidly depleting their funds. As teachers, they each made a dollar an hour, which meant seven dollars a day, $35 a week. Together, they earned a grand total of seventy dollars a week, or $280 a month.

They continued to scrimp and save in myriad ways, but no matter what they saved after rent, food and a few other necessities, $70 a week only went so far. The cabinet worker, George Woods, had to be paid on time. The same was true with the electrician and the plumbers. Smithy no longer had the cash to pay out the amount due to the workers every week. Something had to give. Finally Smithy asked Peter Turczyn and Steve Kovacs if they would consider continuing to work on the house if he gave them $100 a month until he paid them everything he owed. Both men agreed. They felt they had an investment in the project, and working with tremendous dedication six and seven days a week, their hours naturally added up. Turczyn and Kovacs never imagined that the payment would continue, month after month, for the next ten years of their lives, but that is exactly what happened. Over the next ten years —until he paid off every cent—Smithy would never miss a payment.

"If God would grant me a few of the luxuries of life,"
said Frank Lloyd Wright, "I could do without the necessities."

Chapter 14

LET THE LIGHT
SHINE IN

ONE SUNDAY AFTERNOON in the late fall, a desolate Smithy sat alone at the house, assessing what he should do next. The walls were up, the finish cement was laid, the roof was on, and the cabinets were being installed. The house was nearly completed. But there was one glaring exception: there were no windows. And since the back of the house was comprised almost entirely of floor-to-ceiling glass windows and dozens more were positioned throughout the house, this was no small omission.

Smithy had plastic over all the open spaces, but he knew that he soon would have to board them up. He felt sick. Why hadn't he been able to hang on to the amount of money necessary for the purchase and installation of windows? The stockpile he and Sara had built up since the day they were married had dwindled to almost nothing. Now, despite Turczyn and Kovacs' agreement to be paid only $100 a month each, Smithy and Sara had only $500 remaining in their savings account. And that was just a fraction of the $5,000 or more the windows would cost.

Smithy had been hoping to move into the house by the summer holidays, but now there was no chance. No matter how spartan they were willing to be, they couldn't move into a house that had no windows. He would have to board them over and wait until they had saved enough money to purchase the glass. And even if they could afford the glass, they also had to have enough money to pay for cutting and installing it.

Smithy looked at the spaces for the small clerestory windows, the skylights for the kitchen and study, the floor-to-ceiling window spaces, the smaller-sized windows for the two bathrooms and bedrooms. Somehow, it just didn't seem right to board these over, but he had no other option. He was sitting in the living area, wallowing in his sadness, when he heard a knock at the door.

"Come on in," he hollered.

A man dressed in a full-length coat walked in the front door. He introduced himself as Al Taubman and said he was working on a project in Pontiac. "I was at the plaza when this young man mentioned there was a screwy guy building a screwy house out here in Bloomfield Hills," said Taubman. "When I heard that it was designed by Frank Lloyd Wright, I had to come see it for myself. I got directions and came as soon as I could."

Taubman, a developer and a great admirer of Frank Lloyd Wright, clearly was impressed with the workmanship on the house. He walked through it with Smithy, examining the details and agreeing that it was a work of art. Oddly, he somehow seemed to take it personally that a Wright house was being built so nearby his own project without his having a part in it. "Why didn't you contact me to tell me you were building a Frank Lloyd Wright home?" he asked, as if they had previously met or Smithy should have thought of such a thing. "I would certainly have helped. What can I do to help you now? I'll do anything I can."

Smithy had never heard of Taubman and didn't have a clue as to why he would act as if he could have helped to build the house. He did not know that Taubman at that time was on his way to becoming one of the major shopping mall owners in America, and that he would become internationally famous both as a mall builder and owner of Sotheby's. In fact, it never occurred to Smithy that Taubman actually *could* help. As they toured the house, Taubman asked him about the windows and Smithy told him about his problem. He said that he and his family couldn't move into the house as he had hoped because he couldn't buy or install the glass for the windows at this point. He put a good face on it, but as he spoke, Smithy felt swamped by a sense of frustration, knowing that his prospects for successfully completing the house any time soon were nonexistent.

"Don't you worry about it," said Taubman. "I'll send out the Pittsburgh Plate Glass company within the next few days to take the measurements of all your windows. Then they'll install the glass for you when it arrives."

"Oh, no," Smithy protested. "I only have $500, and I know that's not anywhere near the cost."

"Don't you worry about that now."

"But how much will it be?"

"Let's get the windows measured first, then we'll figure out the cost."

The next morning, Monday morning, men from the Pittsburgh Plate Glass Company arrived at Pon Valley Road. They measured all the windows, and then took several days to install all the glass.

It seemed like a miracle.

And, of course to Sara, it was that and more. "God sent an angel to our door," she says. "I knew that our Father would not drop us off in the middle of the street and forget us. We didn't know how, but we both had confidence, trust and reliance that He would take us all the way. I believe that we are always in the right place at the right time, and certainly this event confirmed that belief. Of course, at the time, we didn't know that the man who did such an act of kindness—Alfred Taubman—would become such a successful businessman and eventually one of the wealthiest people in the country. In those days, he didn't have the money he has now, but he was so generous and kind to us."

After the windows were installed, Taubman sent Smithy an invoice for the glass and installation. To Smithy's shock and surprise, the total amount due was just $500, the same amount that Smithy had confided to Taubman that he had left to spend on a few windows. Smithy knew the actual cost was closer to $5000 than to $500, but he paid Taubman's bill with gratitude.

Years later, when Sara and Smithy had to replace a window in one of the small skylights, it cost about $300 for one piece of glass. "Of course that was later," Sara says. "But even so, putting in that glass for such a small amount of money was such a kind gift! I often think of him and the wonderful thing he did for us."

Finally, the construction was finished. Some of the hardware hadn't been installed, but basically the house was ready, and Sara, Smithy and Bobby were eager to move into their beautiful new home. The house had thick heavy doors, beveled windows that cast light across the floor, running water and electricity. When winter came, it would be warmed by radiant heat. In the summers, the house would be cool and comfortable, no matter how hot it was outside.

In its understated simplicity, this house was extraordinary. It was May, 1950, slightly more than a year since construction had begun, when the Smith family moved in. The day over 12 years earlier when Smithy had first seen the photo of Fallingwater that made him declare, "One day I'm going to live in a home designed by Frank Lloyd Wright," and made his classmates roar with laughter, didn't seem that long ago. But here he was. Standing in his own house, his Frank Lloyd Wright house. *Just look at the cupboard doors hung with piano hinges, the brass screws perfectly horizontal. Feel this floor against your bare feet.*

The natural beauty of the house was overwhelming. Everywhere the eye fell was aesthetically pleasing. Each of the two bedrooms, the guest suite (a small bedroom and bathroom), and the study had special features. And the small kitchen was a perfect size for Sara. Built-in shelving, and storage spots under the built-in seating gave them more than enough room for anything they could imagine. Just being in that environment was thrilling. Smithy and Sara were so happy that the fact that they didn't have any money left was not at all daunting to them. Nor was the fact that they didn't have any furniture. Six-year-old Bobby could run out the door and up and down the hills with glee; he loved exploring the rough terrain of his new yard, which seemed almost as big as a park. And he also loved his small, cozy bedroom. Certainly a lack of furniture didn't bother him.

As far as Sara and Smithy were concerned, they had all the essentials: a bridge table and four chairs; their twin beds in their small bedroom; and a mattress for Bobby's bed, set in a boxed structure made of cypress that George Woods had built according to Wright's plan. They also had kitchen supplies—all they needed of pots and pans, plus plates, bowls, cups, glasses, and silverware.

Frank Lloyd Wright had designed a long L-shaped lounge against the entire length of the living room wall, which would serve as a snug sofa and sitting area. Above it, just under the clerestory windows, he'd designed an equally long, built-in shelf that someday would hold an array of hand-crafted ceramics, glass sculptures and other beautiful art objects Sara and Smithy would collect, many from artists at the nearby Cranbrook Academy of Art.

When they moved in, however, Sara and Smithy did not yet have any art, nor did they have cushions or pillows for that seating area or for a lounge in the master bedroom. Frank Lloyd Wright specifically requested that they not put draperies on the windows, which provided solar heat in the winter and a year-round panorama of nature. Nor did he want them to put wall-to-wall rugs on the red leather-like floors. So they would never need draperies or carpeting. Eventually, they wanted to purchase cushions, pillows in the sitting area, and other pieces of furniture. For now, they were happy simply to live in the house—to have this beautiful roof over their heads and to have food to eat and life to enjoy. They both loved their teaching, and Bobby was happy in school. Puttering around his house before and after school, and from dawn to dusk on weekends, filled Smithy with an unmatched happiness. And for Sara, teaching her "auditorium children" at school, directing their performances, coming home to be with Smithy and Bobby, and spending time with her sisters and friends, was abundant satisfaction.

Neither Sara nor Smithy minded cutting corners for their house. They *liked* hot dogs and beans for dinner. And they didn't need to go out dancing; they could dance at home to the tunes of Frank Sinatra on the record player and sing along with popular songs. Movies, which Sara and Smithy both loved, were rarely on their list of activities because they cost too much.

When they did dress up, Smithy looked handsome and Sara, small as she was, always looked chic. Dorie Shwedel, who later married Thelma's son Marvin, remembers how they both managed to look so smart. "Smithy always wore sport jackets, and he was quite dapper," she says. "And Sara always had a flare with what she wore."

Nor did the Smiths lack entertainment. They visited the Afflecks almost every weekend and saw other friends from their childhood, camp and Sunday school days, such as Ben and Lil Chinitz, Irv and Jean Rosen, and Larry and Esther Kunin. They had picnics and meals where they talked and laughed, sang and joked. They still went to Sara's or Smithy's family's homes for Friday night dinners, and often, her sisters or sisters-in-law would send extra food home with Sara that would last her family for two or three nights. Everyone knew that Sara and Smithy didn't have much money, and that whatever they earned, they spent on their home.

"They were over at our house or at the Goldbergs, which was Smithy's sister, Jennie's family, almost every Friday night," recalls Marvin Shwedel, Thelma's son, who was four years older than his cousin Bobby. "That was their socializing. We were out there once a week during the summertime and a couple times a month during the winter. My mother and my aunt were very, very close, as they were with the entire family. We used to have picnics at their home. They had croquet set up, and we always played croquet.

"Aunt Sara made everything fun. She could get out of the real world and go to the fantasy world, and then make parts of that fantasy world real to other people. She made them feel they had an opportunity to reach out and grab onto their fantasies, because she believed in fantasy becoming reality. She believed in your hopes actually coming to fruition.

"She would give people the energy to strive, to reach whatever goals they had. No question about that. She would always say, 'You can do anything you want to do. You have to just have the confidence to go ahead and do it. If you think you can do it, you *can* do it.' She didn't believe in impossibilities. She believed in possibilities."

Both Sara and Smithy had a positive attitude about what they had and didn't have. Smithy often quoted Thoreau, who said, "Make yourself rich by making your wants few," and that is just what they did. At the same time, they felt in tune with something Frank Lloyd Wright himself had said during a period when he had very few, if any, commissions: "If God would grant me a few of the luxuries of life, I could do without the necessities."

Living in that house—in such a remarkable space, surrounded by such a serene, artistic environment—was in itself a luxury beyond imagination. Just walking through the front door into a darkened hallway and turning into the light-filled living room was thrilling. Sara and Smithy often found themselves surprised and excited all over again as they turned the corner from the low ceiling of the entranceway—where Smithy at 5'5" could actually touch the ceiling—into the open living room with its high sloping ceiling and 16-foot-tall wall of floor-to-ceiling glass that filled the room with light and opened on to a stunning panorama of the changing seasons. The clean line of the red terra cotta floors, the expansiveness of what could be deemed a small space, seemed to open new vistas in every way.

"We've been constantly amazed by the feeling of living in this house," Smithy would later say. "Although I've turned the corners thousands of times, I look forward to turning them again and again. It's like being in the woods and wondering what's beyond the tree that looms before you."

Waking up and going to sleep in those spaces was extraordinary. The family was inhabiting a living, nearly breathing, sculpture designed by Frank Lloyd Wright. "He has made me feel like a giant on earth," Smithy said in an interview later in his life. "So many people say Wright's architecture overwhelms them, but this house doesn't dominate me. I'm continually delighted by the visual excitement and intrigue." The cypress alone, with its honey-colored tones, was wonderful to see and to touch. Wright had specified cypress, which is sometimes referred to as "the wood eternal," not only because of its wonderful color, but also because it has an interior chemistry that makes it rot-proof and vermin-proof. So not only was the cypress visually warm and beautiful, it also emitted a quality of endurance and strength that gave it a feeling of the essence of nobility.

Many years later, in 1979, when a panel from the American Institute of Architects judged the Smith home as one of the 50 most beautiful structures in the six-county area of Southeastern Michigan—one of only two private homes included in the AIA's 50 selections—Smithy would tell a reporter: "To me it's a piece of sculpture. Space flows to space. At no point is there a boxed-in feeling. Frank Lloyd Wright had a remarkable understanding of human scale. He recognized that a house or building can be an embellishment of nature and environment. It's one house for a lifetime."

Sara and Smithy's friends and family were thrilled for them when they first moved into their house. But not everyone was equally happy about the Smiths' move into their new house on Pon Valley Road. One family, in fact, was furious about it. Unbeknownst to Sara and Smithy as they went so joyfully about their business, one couple who lived nearby were quite determined to get Sara and Smithy out of their dream house and out of the neighborhood. The reason was simple. It had come to their attention that the Smiths were Jews. And from their perspective, Jews had no business being able to buy property in that neighborhood, let alone live there. This was a white Anglo-Saxon Protestant neighborhood, and the only thing as bad as having Blacks move into the neighborhood was having Jews. No doubt, the presence of Jews meant that property values would drop; standards would cease to exist.

Years later, Bob Smith would talk about the 1950's drama that had unfolded behind the scenes in the affluent area around their home: "All of our neighbors were fairly wealthy," Bob says. "They were either automobile company executives or people who had inherited a lot of money. A few weeks after we moved in, our neighbors, the Griswolds, told all of the other neighbors that Jews had moved into this community, and they asked for support in trying to drive us out. They decided to take a petition around the neighborhood asking us to leave the area.

"One of the Griswolds' first stops with their petition was at the home of the most prominent family in the area, the Fisher family. This Fisher was Everell Fisher, the son of Charles T. Fisher, who with his brothers started Fisher Body Company and became the largest shareholder in General Motors. Apparently, when General Motors bought Fisher Body, they paid most of the price in stock. So at that time, the Fisher brothers and their families were worth hundreds of millions of dollars, which was something almost unheard of in those days."

After calling first to see if they could stop by, the Griswolds arrived at the Fishers, where Everell and Susan Fisher invited them into the liv-ing room. As the story was later related, the Griswolds got right to the point, and said something to the effect of: "We have a problem here. These people should not have been sold this piece of property. There was a restriction in this deed of property saying Jews would **not** be allowed to own this land. But despite that, it was sold! And now they've built this house! And it's a crazy house. We don't want them in this com-munity. What we're asking you to do is to sign a petition that tells them we want them to get out of there."

Susan Fisher said, "Let me see that petition."

The Griswolds handed it to her. She looked it over, and then, in front of them, she ripped it up. Tore it into little pieces.

"Listen," she said, "if you try this again, I will take every dollar I have, and I will fight you personally. Nobody is going to do this to another human being if I can help it. I don't even know who these peo-ple are, but now I'm going to go over and I'm going to introduce myself. I'm going to invite them into my house. And they have a little son over there, right?"

"Yes."

"Well, I want you to know that this kid is going to be at my house, and my house is going to be his house, and I don't ever want to hear one word against them again."

Susan Fisher's declaration, as it turned out, was the end of the issue. The Griswolds gave up their fight against the Smiths.

And that afternoon, Susan Fisher sent her nanny over to the Smiths to invite Bobby to come play with her children. The Smiths' house was very close by, only a couple of acres away, on the other side of Pon Valley Road. It was the first of many afternoons that Bobby spent at the Fishers' home. Soon, a steady path was worn down between both houses.

"We became lifelong friends," says Bob. "They became my second family. I was always at the Fishers' house. Always. Their daughter, Susan, and their son, Peter, became my closest childhood friends. In fact, Peter was in my wedding 21 years after this event. I just love that family and the values they represented. Ironically, even the Griswolds became our friends. When Mrs. Griswold's husband passed away, she

often would ask Mom to stay over with her to keep her company at
night. It's clear that their initial prejudice came from ignorance and
fear, but I will never forgot what Mrs. Fisher did for our family. It was
just incredible."

"Mrs. Fisher and her family were very special people," Bob continues. "Susan Fisher was a Briggs—and her family owned the Detroit
Tigers and built Briggs Stadium. Her sister, Jane Briggs Hart, was married to Phil Hart, who eventually became Senator Hart, the person after
whom they named the Senate Office Building. Senator Hart was nominated for the Supreme Court, but he would not accept, because, as he
said to President Johnson, 'If you don't get reelected, I think the new
president should have a chance to select a Chief Justice.' On a personal
note, Phil Hart was one of the first people to encourage me to go into
public service, but he always joked with me not to run for election
against him, to wait until he retired.

"Jane Hart, Phil's wife and Aunt Jane to me, also had great convic-
tion and courage. She was the only Senate wife to be arrested on the
steps of the Pentagon for protesting the U.S. invasion in Cambodia. She
was a pilot and the first woman to be selected as an astronaut by NASA.
You have to understand, this is the family that Susan Fisher came from.
That wonderful family—Susan, Phil and Aunt Jane—had a great impact
on my moral and social consciousness that would influence me for the
rest of my life."

Sara and Smithy had been rescued once again, but the threat, and
the rescue, barely registered on the barometer of their happiness at
being in their new home. Their daily pleasure was immense. They loved
every time of day in their house—the mornings, the afternoons, the
evenings, the night. The Afflecks visited them and in turn invited them
to a breakfast with Bill and Mary Palmer, who were building a Frank
Lloyd Wright home in Ann Arbor. Bill, an economics professor, and
Mary, a musician and teacher, showed Sara and Smithy Wright's plans
for their home, which was set on a hillside in the midst of an apple
orchard. Wright had chosen to base his design of the Palmer's home on
an equilateral triangle. This meant that there were no right angles in the

entire house. The open living room with its panoramic views of the hill-side apple-orchard, had a peaked cypress-wood ceiling formed by three triangles, and the floor tiles were equal-sided triangles of terra cotta tiles. The Palmers moved into their home in 1952, and over the years, they often spent time with the Smiths and the Afflecks over meals and coffee, swapping Frank Lloyd Wright stories and comparing details and impressions they had about living in and maintaining their wonderfully aesthetic homes.

As Mary Palmer would later say, "Our house has been one of the most major influences of my life in every way." This was true for each of the Frank Lloyd Wright homeowners, who all had the experience of being a part of nature by simply looking out of their living room windows. Mary spoke for all of them when she said, "This house has influenced how I appreciate these trees, how I appreciate the way the land falls off, how I appreciate music. It's just been an enriching of every artistic impulse I've ever had. It isn't something that hits you and then is done. It continues. It's a living thing.

"These houses are treasures; they're works of art. It's not something like a painting that can be hung in a museum, where you regulate the temperature and then it's done. You're on the edge of something inside or outside, something that's happening all the time."

By intentional destruction of the box as the basis of building, we open the road to a great future architecture. This secret is not my secret. It is the age-old philosophy of individuality—the entire core of the creative self, the entire spiritual world, which you may enter only by way of love of it, which is the greatest understanding, after all. Now, be both patient and wise, and you can't miss the integrity of this innate, inside thing. See it operating in nature everywhere. Go afield. Go along with or go against your fellow man. Go anywhere you please with eyes open to see. Ask this troublesome question, 'Why?' And if you have a sincere wish to learn, it's a kind of prayer.

—*Frank Lloyd Wright, 1952*

Chapter 15

NEW VISTAS:
Living in the Light

ONE BRILLIANT WINTER MORNING when Sara and Smithy woke up, they saw tracks in the fresh snow and nose prints on the glass of the living room windows, left by people looking in the night before. The nose prints made them laugh. From the time they moved in, long before the house had furniture, it had visitors. Hundreds of them. Students of architecture stopped by, along with Frank Lloyd Wright aficionados, curiosity seekers, old friends and neighbors. Dr. Betsy Jane Welling, the Wayne State University professor who first introduced Smithy to Wright's designs in her graduate humanities course, had brought her students out to see the house during its construction, and now she brought them to see the finished product.

When Sam Frank, a friend Smithy met at Wayne State after the war, first brought his mother out to see the house, she gave Sara and Smithy a small leather-bound guest book as a housewarming gift, and within the first week, dozens and dozens of names began lining the pages. Interested passers by—many of whom had never heard of Frank Lloyd Wright—were drawn by the unusual shape of the house, by the setting, by the golden glow it cast during the night. Often they stopped, looked, and knocked on the door. If Sara and Smithy were home, they always invited the visitors in to look around and to sign the guest book. Eventually that guest book would contain thousands of names, along with their comments about the house: "Enchanting!" "What a lovely home!" "Peaceful." "Beautiful!" "Magnificent." "Thank you, thank you. I had a *fabulous* time."

Having so many visitors wasn't always convenient. For instance, when Bobby was growing up, he would often take a bath early in the morning, and on any number of occasions, he would look up from the tub and see two or three people looking at him through the window. Since there were no curtains, there was no guarantee of privacy. Another inconvenience was that people always felt free to ring the doorbell. They rang during lunches, they rang during dinners. But no matter how inconvenient it was, no matter what time they came, they were always graciously welcomed and invited to see the house.

One time a couple from Brazil set up camp across the road from the house. When Sara realized that they had been walking around the house for at least two days, she told Smithy, and he strode across the street and greeted them. The campers explained that they were traveling around the country looking at Frank Lloyd Wright homes.

"Well, what are you out here for?" Smithy said. "Please come in! I'll take you for a tour of the house, and you can join us for dinner."

Sara never seemed in the least distressed by surprise visitors. She welcomed them with open arms. (As one of her friends said, "Never would anybody welcome you like Sara. Love is her thing. She is the most hospitable person in the world.") The Brazilian couple, who had been traveling around the country looking at Frank Lloyd Wright houses, seemed enchanted. After dinner around the table with Sara, Smithy and Bobby, Smithy invited them to stay overnight. Many other visitors were welcomed just as warmly, whether for an hour, an afternoon or a weekend.

"Dad didn't want people just looking from the outside," Bob remembers. "He wanted them in the house so that he could tell them his story. When anyone stopped by, it meant at least an hour-long lecture. He was so happy talking about the house. And when he told his story, he was like a maestro with an orchestra. You could see the excitement in his eyes. He was unbelievable.

"It was as if he was a teacher in his own house, trying to teach people to understand and appreciate Frank Lloyd Wright as an architect. He'd tell them how Wright's architectural theories applied to his house, how he had learned about Frank Lloyd Wright, and how he and Mom met with Wright on their first visit to Taliesin. It was fascinating. And Mom and I would sit there and play our parts. He was a master at it. He was mesmerizing. Watching him as a kid, I could not believe that anybody could love anything so much in their life as he loved the house. I loved his passion. I guess you could resent it or you could admire it, and I admired it. I learned from it."

Smithy's unbridled enthusiasm for Frank Lloyd Wright was echoed by the intensity and energy he put into his teaching. Smithy always arrived at school early in the morning, and, as a dance teacher and sponsor of the yearbook, he stayed late. In the first and second grades, Bob attended Longfellow Elementary, his mother's school. But in the third grade, he switched to Everett Elementary, which was next to Cody High, where his dad taught. Every morning at 7:30, Smithy and Bob would drop off Sara at Marsh Elementary, where she was now teaching, and then drive to Cody High School. Bob would sit in the teachers' lounge with his dad and "watch the teachers smoke and curse" for about 20 minutes. When his dad started to teach class, he would walk the short distance across the playing fields to his own school, where class started at 9 a.m. When school got out, he would walk back to Cody High, where once or twice a week he would watch Smithy teaching ballroom dancing classes.

Throughout his childhood and as he got older, Bob observed his father's classroom teaching. Bob also sat in on many of the hours when Smithy and his students were working on the yearbook. Smithy's yearbook students walked away with national prizes year after year, and watching how hard they all worked, Bob understood why. In the process, he witnessed the respect and affection the students showed his father.

"He taught from his heart," Bob says. "He taught literature. But he really taught people about life. To this day, people who know who I am will say to me, 'Your dad was the greatest teacher I've ever had. He changed my life. He taught me to appreciate things I never would have appreciated.'

"You know, just as he had his stories about Frank Lloyd Wright, he had his stories about Shakespeare. And he read poetry beautifully. He interpreted poetry and made you think about it in a new way. One guy—a stranger—came up to me on the street one time and said, 'I was basically a hoodlum until your dad taught me Shakespeare, and that changed my life forever.'"

Smithy also was famous with his friends and family for his word play. He loved puns. His niece, Dorie Shwedel, was one of Smithy's biggest fans. "I love words," says Dorie, who was an advertising copywriter when she first knew Smithy. "Words always captivated me, as they did Smithy. So, when he would deliver his puns, there would be these groans. But I loved them. They were so clever. And I remember, he always laughed at his own jokes, even if no one else did. He was brilliant in how he used and played with words."

But however much Smithy loved language and teaching, his first love was the house. "He always found time to go out and throw footballs and baseballs with me," Bob says, "and he would always come to watch me play sports. There wasn't any question; he would be there. At the same time, any free moment he had, he was back at home.

"This was a man who jumped out of bed on the weekends because he could be with his house," says Bob. "And, I mean, he would enjoy the most simple tasks. When we first built the house, we couldn't afford any landscaping, so he cleared the land himself. He chopped down trees. And he helped clear the marsh. That piece of property was gorgeous, but it was a rough gem; there were marshes over half the property. So he had to slowly trim back the trees, trim back the marsh, and control that vegetation.

"Most people get up and say, 'Oh, my God, I've got work to do around the house; let me get this done so I can enjoy myself.' But he loved working around his house. People would say, 'But Melvyn, you don't have any new clothes, you never take trips, you don't go to parties, you don't travel to Europe, you don't. . . .' And he would say, 'I don't need all that. I have everything I want here—everything. I can't go to Europe and find what I don't have here. I can't go to a party and find what I don't have here. I'm outside. I'm with nature. I have work clothes and the clothes I need to go to class—that's all that matters. I will do without necessities so I can have my dream.' And that was it.

"Both Mom and I understood that the house was his first priority. We didn't take that personally. We were happy for him. We knew this was his heaven. I have chosen a different balance in my own life. But I will always appreciate the fact that he taught me how to be passionate about the things you love."

When Bob started fifth grade, his parents finally let him take the bus to and from his neighborhood school (Vaughn School) by himself, and so he began to arrive home before his father. "I would watch Dad come home," Bob says, "and I would see him walk around outside. He looked at the property as an artist would look at his painting to see what he wanted to do next. He would study the landscaping. He would gaze at the house, and at times he almost seemed like a cat prowling after its prey, walking in judgement. You know how a cat looks at a little bird or something, and then crouches down a little? Well, you'd see Dad, all of a sudden, react in a certain way as he was looking at things. He was always visualizing, always imagining—whether it was a Japanese tea house or Japanese garden that he someday wanted to build or how the reflections of light against a man-made lake would look. It was every moment.

"And that intensity was in everything he did, including this lawn that we always kept clean. When I was a kid, weeding was one of my jobs, and he would come out and say, 'Okay, there are too many weeds here.' We would basically be weeding a lawn, which was not a beautifully sodded lawn because he couldn't afford sod. And if you broke off the weed without getting the roots, the weed would grow again. So, he would come around and check to see how much of the roots I had gotten because he was a perfectionist.

"Everything he did, from pulling weeds to picking up branches that had fallen during a windstorm, had to be done as perfectly as possible. This was a work of art, and every day he wanted the house and grounds to be beautiful. Picking weeds or cleaning up the fallen branches didn't cost a lot, but it always improved the picture. He would be trimming a tree, and he would get down and look at it, and then he'd go back and he'd cut it some more. You would think he was shaping a sculpture. And he was."

Recalling the way Smithy worked, Sara says, "Smithy cut over two hundred trees, and he didn't do it with an electric saw. He did it with a hand saw because he couldn't afford to hire anyone to do it for him, and he couldn't afford expensive tools, so he would use the cheapest thing. Oh, I can't tell you how hard he worked. And he did beautiful work. Absolutely beautiful."

Both Sara and Bob saw that even though Smithy often worked to exhaustion, he loved every minute of it. "At the end of the day, he was almost sad to come in," Bob remembers. "He couldn't get enough of it. Whatever he was doing outside was adding to the beauty of the place. And that was day in, day out, year after year, decade after decade, until he was so sick that he could hardly do it any more. Even then, he would sit on his John Deere tractor and cut the lawn because he could still do that. When he drove that tractor around, he would sit high—as if he were driving a Rolls Royce. It would take three to four hours to cut all the grass on the property. So, for those hours, he would see everything." Surveying his kingdom.

Shortly after the first anniversary of their move into Pon Valley Road, the interior of the their house was greatly enhanced with comfortable places for friends and visitors to sit. That's because Irving Goldberg, Jennie's husband, gave them an unparalleled housewarming gift—a maple wood dining room table, eight low-backed maple wood chairs, two coffee tables, and six hassocks, all designed by Frank Lloyd Wright. The long rectangular table actually could be detached to form three separate tables if the occasion called for that kind of arrangement. Irving had asked the master carpenters who worked in his showcase business to make all of this furniture according to Wright's plan. Wright had designed this furniture, all of it extraordinarily beautiful, to be complementary to the free-flowing grid of the house. The geometric planes of the furniture also contrasted with the jagged pattern of the recessed lighting grids in the dining room.

"We were so thrilled," Sara remembers. "It was such a beautiful gift from Irv and Jennie." The Wright furniture not only was complementary to the grid, but it added a dignity and elegance to the interior that the bridge table and folding chairs had not been able to bestow.

Because they were paying off Peter Turczyn and Steve Kovaks and other craftsmen who had been working on their house, Smithy and Sara still didn't have money to buy cushions for the built-in seating areas in the living room and bedroom. But one evening when they were at Thelma's, they met a neighbor of Thelma's who was in the sail cloth business. They asked his advice about cushions, and he ended up offering to make the cushions himself at a great discount. Within a very short time, he had covered cushions with green sail cloth for the built-in sofa for their living room and made a cushion of terra-cotta red sail cloth for the master bedroom. He also covered extra pillows for the living room lounge in green and red sail cloth, which is a sturdy and long-lasting material, and he made comfortable green bottom cushions for the dining room chairs. These items were early entries into what eventually would be a home filled with handcrafted furniture, weavings and a wide variety of sculpture and paintings. It was a home that would be the site of concerts, weddings, impromptu plays and theater productions. But it happened slowly, one step at a time.

Shortly after they received their new Wright-designed furniture from the Goldbergs, Sara and Smithy learned exciting news. Frank Lloyd Wright himself was going to be lecturing in Detroit. Wright often came to Michigan because, of his hundreds of buildings throughout the United States, 33 were located in Michigan, from Marquette in the upper penninsula, to Ann Arbor, to Grosse Isle, near the mouth of the Detroit River. Illinois, the only other Midwestern state to surpass the number of buildings, mostly homes, designed by Frank Lloyd Wright, had 99 such structures.

Frank Lloyd Wright drew large audiences wherever he went. Even though the brilliance of his architecture, his vision and his genius would seem even more extraordinary in retrospect, at the time he occupied a rarified space in the popular imagination. His coming to Detroit to speak was electrifying. But what made this visit absolutely astounding to the Smiths was the fact that after his lecture, Mr. Wright wanted to meet with Sara and Smithy and to see their home on Pon Valley Road.

The morning after his lecture, Frank Lloyd Wright himself would travel to Bloomfield Hills, to My Haven, to see how his design had turned out.

Sara and Smithy, of course, cleaned the house to perfection. Every surface and every wall shone before they eagerly drove to his lecture. They took along Bob, who still remembers the experience vividly. "The man's mind was probably one of the five or ten greatest minds of the twentieth century," he says now. "Absolutely incredible. I remember that *The New York Times* had taken him on, they were criticizing him, and he said, 'How can I get all upset about *The New York Times* criticizing my architecture when the next day it's used to wrap fish?'

"After his talk," Bob says, "he shook my hand, and he said, 'You know, if here was a hill, an architect would put a house on top of the hill.' He put the knuckles of one fist on top of the other. 'But I integrate them,' he continued, separating his fingers and interlocking them. 'The hill and the house become one, nature is enhanced with my house, and my house is enhanced by nature.'"

The following morning when Wright came out to Bloomfield Hills to visit the Smith's home, he seemed very pleased with what he saw. He walked all around, examining the details, noticing the precision with which his plans had been carried out. Then he stood in the living room, looked around and said, "This is my little gem."

"He told Smithy, 'I will give you a plaque to put on your house,'" Sara recalls. "Apparently Wright did not give these plaques out to many of the people who built his buildings—only to the clients who had executed his plans in the way he directed. But he thought Smithy had earned it."

During that first visit, Frank Lloyd Wright, dressed in his trademark attire of an impeccable white three-piece suit, white shoes and cape, stopped in front of a brass lamp hanging down from the ceiling, looked at it, raised his cane and tapped the lamp two or three times. "Smith," he said. "Replace this lamp." He touched the cypress walls and studied the way the light fell on the rectilinear fireplace. He sat on the built-in couch and gazed out of the floor-to-ceiling windows toward the marshland in the back. Later on, he sat down again—this time in a canvas wing chair in the livingroom that was both deep and somewhat uncomfortable. When it came time to leave, he had a lot of difficulty lifting himself out of the chair. Smithy helped him stand up.

"That chair is going outside as soon as I can replace it," Smithy said.

"Better make sure it goes way outside," Wright responded with a chuckle.

Over the years, Sara and Smithy took their son with them to several of Wright's lectures. Bob remembers those events, as well as the three times Wright visited their Pon Valley Road home. "Frank Lloyd Wright didn't just have ideas about architecture," Bob recalls. "He had a view of how we need to live together. One time someone in the audience asked, 'Why do you make the bedrooms so small?' And he said, 'Because I want to force people to get up and get out of their bedrooms, so that they go and interact with each other. I want the family to interact with each other in the living room. I want them to have meals together. I want them to share music together. I want them to talk about books together. I don't want them to go in their bedrooms and hide.' He designed a house based on this structure of what he felt the family should be, what he felt culture should be."

Wright visited his "little gem"—which Wright's apprentices consider one of the finest examples of his Usonian homes—two more times before his death in 1959. Once in 1953 and once in 1957. In 1953, Sara and Smithy were looking forward to going into Detroit to hear Wright give a lecture for senior citizens. Mary Palmer, who was living with her husband and children in their Frank Lloyd Wright house in Ann Arbor, called the organizers the day before the lecture to ask them where they were planning on having their luncheon after the talk. Usually the people who organized the lecture also gave a luncheon, and the Palmers, Smiths and Afflecks all wanted to attend. Living in homes designed by Frank Lloyd Wright gave them not only an affinity for Frank Lloyd Wright but a bond with each other as well.

When the organizers told Mary Palmer that they hadn't planned any lunch at all, the three women decided to host an event themselves. "Mary called me and Elizabeth Affleck and we decided to have a luncheon at my house," Sara says. "I had just been to the store and I had bought a whole lot of corn on the cob and much more fish than I could possibly use in a week. When I bought it, I thought 'Why am I buying so much corn? Why so much fish?' but I bought it anyway, and that Saturday night, I realized it was for the luncheon.

"In those days, we didn't have supermarkets open on Sundays, and so whatever we had was what we had to use. Mary said, 'I've got a shoulder lamb that I have frozen; I'll just take that out of the freezer and cook it, and of course I'll bring a big salad.' Elizabeth Affleck said, 'I'll make dessert. I can make peach cobbler and also bring a salad.'

"We were able to have a lovely luncheon," Sara remembers. "We set the food out on the table and invited Mr. Wright to go to the buffet first. He said that one of his favorite foods was corn on the cob, and he helped himself and came over here to the built-in lounge. We had tables set up along the lounge, and as I said, the lounge can seat 20 to 25 people, depending on their size. Anyway, Frank Lloyd Wright was sitting toward the end of the lounge alone and no one came near him. No one was talking to him. Then he said, 'Isn't anyone going to sit with me?'

"So some people moved in. But they didn't stay. They would go over and say a word or two and walk away. People just don't seem to want to go up to a genius or a great person. I don't know whether it's fear or something else.

"At the time, I was in the kitchen taking care of the dishes, and the thought came to me, 'Sara, you're doing a Mary-Martha.' In the Bible story, Martha was the one who always stayed in the kitchen mumbling and grumbling because Mary didn't help her. Well, there I was in the kitchen pulling a Mary-Martha, and the thought came, 'What are you doing in the kitchen? Get in there and talk to that man.' So I did. I dried my hands and went over and sat down with him, and he talked to me about how he could tell the time of day and the season of the year by the shadows on the walls. He talked about all the things that shadows told him." Wright told her how the house was laid out on angles that took advantage of the seasons and the position of the sun, utilizing solar energy to help heat the house in the winter and keep it cool in the summers. Wright also told Sara how the way shadows fell on the walls had given him insight into how best to take advantage of the sun's energy and make this happen.

"It was very interesting," she says, "and I was so grateful that I had gone over to sit with him. While we were talking, I asked him, 'Mr. Wright, what do you consider to be the greatest design you ever made?' His reply was 'Why, the next one.'"

Between Wright's visits to Detroit and Bloomfield Hills, the Smiths went to Spring Green on a few different occasions. On one of Smithy and Sara's visits to Taliesin, Frank Lloyd Wright beckoned for them to step into a little room with him. Inside the room, he reached up on a shelf and took down a small red plaque—the promised plaque that was, in essence, Wright's seal of approval. The plaque, made of ceramic and about two inches by six inches, was dusty. Wright wiped it off on his pants and ceremoniously handed it to Smithy.

"Smithy wrapped it in cotton batting, and he didn't put it on the house right away," Sara says. "He took such good care of that plaque. But one day he decided that finally this was the day to put up his Frank Lloyd Wright plaque. Just as he was going to morter it in, it dropped and broke in half. Well, Smithy was devastated, but he took the plaque very carefully and put it back together again. There is just a tiny seam there, but I always used to tease him that we had a cracked Frank Lloyd Wright home."

*"Gratitude is riches, and we have so much to be
grateful for,"* says Sara.

Chapter 16

THE FINISHING TOUCHES:
A Landscape of Love

During Frank Lloyd Wright's visit in 1957, Smithy talked to him about future plans for the house that included the possible addition of a garden room, as well as landscaping for the property. Even though the marshy pond and the trees on the land had a natural charm, Smithy had a lot more in mind. He wanted a beautiful landscape that included a Japanese garden, as well as a larger, deeply dug lake instead of a marshy pond with cattails growing out of it. His fantasy was to have the famous American landscape architect Thomas Church design his gardens. Church, who was based in San Francisco, often had worked on large commercial and institutional projects, but his genius for domestic-scale garden designs that were sensitive to the environment had drawn Smithy's interest and admiration. Church was known for his responsiveness to his clients' values and lifestyles, and he liked clients to use and enjoy their gardens, not just admire them from afar as his own artistic or social statement.

One Sunday afternoon in the the early 1960s, a group of men from the Midland Dow Chemical Plant came to visit the house. Smithy gave them a tour and told them the story of how it happened that Frank Lloyd Wright had agreed to design the house. Afterwards, he walked outside and stood talking with them in the wide, curving driveway that led from Pon Valley Road up to the house. Smithy looked around and apologized about the appearance of the grounds. "I'm waiting until I can afford to have Thomas Church do my landscaping," he said.

The young men from Dow Chemical started to laugh, which startled Smithy. "Why are you laughing?" he asked. They said the coincidence struck them as funny: at that moment, Thomas Church was meeting with Dow at Midland, and he wasn't planning on going back to New York until Tuesday. They just happened to have the telephone number where Church could be reached.

As soon as the young men left, Smithy called Thomas Church. He told Church, "I can't afford you, but I have a Frank Lloyd Wright house, and I would love to have you consider doing the landscaping." Church, apparently drawn to the idea of doing the landscaping for a Wright home, said that as soon as he was done with the job he was doing on Monday afternoon, he would come out and spend some time with Smithy.

"Dad was so excited he could hardly sleep at night," Bob remembers. "He was just so thrilled to have this guy here. He said, 'I have the world's best architect, and now I want the world's best landscape architect.'"

Which is how it came to be that the renowned Thomas Church spent a day trudging around My Haven with Smithy in 1957. Apparently Church was captivated by Smithy's stories of his life and his relationship with Frank Lloyd Wright. Bob remembers his saying, "Your enthusiasm is unbelievable. I rarely see it."

Church was wearing his boots, and during and after the time they walked around the land, he began sketching out a design on a piece of onion skin paper and making notes on the landscaping. As they walked, he talked about his ideas with Smithy. At the end of the day, he said, "Okay, now, if I take this plan back to my office with me and send it back to you perfectly rendered, it'll cost you thousands of dollars. But if I give this to you now, all it will cost you is a good dinner."

Sara had prepared a spaghetti dinner for Mr. Church, and during the meal she listened as Thomas Church and Smithy talked about the design Church had just handed to Smithy. "We were eating dinner in the living room and facing out on the grounds," Sara says. "Mr. Church was looking at the grounds, and he said that when he created 'the swirl,' he would remove that little oak tree."

Normally, Sara let Smithy call the shots on the decisions about such things, but this time she intervened. "Oh, Mr. Church, you aren't going to cut down my little oak tree!" she cried out. "Please don't cut it down."

"Well," he said, "I am sure I can create my swirl and leave the tree there."

Sara was relieved and gratified. (Years later, that tree would turn out to be the most important tree on the property. It would provide much needed shade in the summer to the grounds next to the house. Also, Smithy hung a wicker swing from one of its strongest branches, and every summer, he would swing his grandchildren there.)

Church stayed overnight, and he was up early the next morning tromping around the grounds with Smithy close by his side. After several hours, he came back inside and used the dining room table as a drafting board. When he had completed writing out further plans, he handed them to Smithy and got ready to leave. "Smithy asked him what the bill was," Sara says. "Mr. Church got a twinkle in his eye. I think he could see by the furnishings that we did not have much money. And he said, 'Well, you see, I was a guest in your home and I enjoyed our camaraderie so much that this is my price.' The amount he requested was so small that Smithy was able to make him out a check for the full amount right then and there."

After he left, Church sent Smithy and Sara a copy of his highly-praised book on landscaping, *Gardens Are for People,* with the following inscription:

> *To The Melvyn Smiths—*
> *1 Fine House*
> *2 Splendid Acres*
> *3 Nice people and a*
>   *lot of beautiful oaks.*
>   *What am I doing here?*
> *Thomas D. Church*
> *November 1957*

And so it was that with Church's landscape designs in hand, Smithy set about executing the flowing lines of Church's plans for the gardens, the pond and the rest of the landscaping. Church had specified plant-

ing certain trees in certain spots, and he told Smithy what kind of trees
to buy first and when and where to plant them. Smithy bought oak,
willow, yellow birch, flowering crab and Austrian pines—and he didn't
buy tiny trees. He bought full grown trees—initially alarming Sara
with the costs and creating one of the only disputes anyone remembers
their having.

Smithy also created all the beds for flowers and bushes, with flat
juniper, wisteria, azalea and rhododendron, according to Thomas D.
Church design. He also had told Church how much he wanted a
Japanese garden, and so Church had designed a pretty little Japanese
garden for him. Someday, Smithy said, he would build a Japanese
tea house near that garden, and they could go out and sit in it for afternoon tea.

Years later, Roy Slade, the President of the Cranbrook Academy of
Art, which was just down the road from the Smiths' home, would say
that anyone walking around the Melvyn Maxwell and Sara Smith house
and grounds could see "the integration of art, architecture and nature."
He recalled a recent visit and said, "In this house, one sees that harmony is fully realized . . . As Melvyn took you around these grounds, he
was like a conductor, orchestrating all the elements, as indeed they were
orchestrated by Frank Lloyd Wright. His enthusiasm, understanding
and sensitivity came through in his words and wisdom. As we circled
the house, he pointed out details, harmonies and placements with
enthusiasm and expertise . . . fully feeling the totality of the integration
of architecture and nature as they're expressed in this house and in
these surroundings."

Living in their house was in itself an experience that enhanced all
aspects of artistic awareness in both Smithy and Sara. In Smithy, it
brought out a love of art that manifested itself in his work on his house
and in a new occupation of searching out and supporting the work of
young artists. As he beautified the outside, he also began collecting art
to enhance the interior with the kind of random scattering of art objects
he so admired at Taliesen—a statue here, a sculpture there, a piece of
pottery, a tapestry. He and Sara began visiting galleries and art exhibits

My Haven: A view from the dining room into the living room.

The living room flows into the dining room, and the floor-to-ceiling windows
make nature's changing seasons part of the daily panorama.

The garden room, added in the 1970s, is separated from the dining room by a wall screen that echoes the design of the windows.

ABOVE: In autumn, the west side of the house after the addition of the garden room and study.

OPPOSITE, TOP: The north side of the house in winter. BOTTOM: The west side of the house in the winter of 2000.

The living room holds specially designed Wright coffee tables and hassocks.

ABOVE: Side view of the house. BELOW: The house and terrace from the south in summer.

Mike Calligan's large "natural bridge" sculpture in front of the house.

in their area—at the Detroit Art Institute, the Artists' Market and galleries in Birmingham and Southfield. Almost always, they went to the
various exhibits by artists at the Cranbrook Art Institute, which was just
up the road.

Slowly but surely, they began to collect pottery, glass, sculptures
and other art objects. Every piece of art in their house had a story,
beginning with a piece of beveled glass they were given by a couple of
artists who were moving to Florida. Smithy and Sara had taken the glass
home, where Smithy put it in one of the window spaces. "Smithy liked
it so much that he said 'Sara, let's go right back and ask them if they will
make a stained glass pane for that set of windows and one for the other
side of the table,'" Sara recalls. "So we did go right back and they said
they were moving their kiln within a very short time, but they would try
to do it for us. And so they did. At night we would put the light on it and
it looked beautiful.

"Smithy was an adventurer. He and I would go into a gallery, and I
would admire things, but he would see things right away that he knew
he wanted." Sara estimates that three out of every four pieces of art in
their house came from Cranbrook, and that often, even if the piece
wasn't purchased at Cranbrook, they later would learn that the artist
had been a Cranbrook student."

One afternoon early in their lives as art collectors, Sara and Smithy
went to an exhibit on Impressionism at the Cranbrook Art Institute and
then decided to stop by the Englander Furniture store and its adjoining
store, the American House, which only sold original handcrafted art. As
they were walking down the steps into the American House, they saw a
group of people crowded around something. "Smithy said, 'Let's go see
what they're looking at,'" Sara said. "As we walked over, we saw this
magnificent handcrafted chest, and the sun was shining down on the
chest and lighting up the copper and the gold, and yellow and red colors.
They had some tea cups and saucers sitting on top. And Smithy looked
at it and said, 'Oh how I wish we could have this! This piece belongs in
our home.' I also wished we could have it, and we went over to talk to
Joyce, the manager of America House. We knew Joyce well because Smithy
had already purchased many small art pieces there, and she had been to

our house. When we walked up to Joyce, she said, 'Smithy, that piece belongs in your home.' Smithy said, 'I agree. We love that piece! What is the price?' I don't remember the amount she quoted, but it was very expensive. Smithy said, 'That's impossible, Joyce. We can't afford it.'"

As they were leaving, Joyce called out "Yes, but you should have it in your home. It belongs there."

Sara says that she and Smithy went on to the Detroit Institute of Art to see an exhibit of Renoir, and all the way there they talked about that chest. Not only was it beautiful, but it also could act as a storage area, which was something they could use. They wanted it in their home, but they had no idea how they could afford it. "Usually Smithy had answers for every problem, but not this time," Sara says. "We got to the exhibit and hadn't even begun to look at the paintings when all of a sudden Smithy said, 'Sara, when people want something and they don't have enough money to purchase it, they pay so much down and so much a month. Maybe we ought to put a down payment on this piece and pay so much a month . . .'

"So with that idea, we just flew out of the Art Institute. We ran down the stairs and into the car because we wanted to get to the American House before they closed at 5 p.m. When Joyce saw us, we were shaking our heads 'Yes,' and she said, 'Oh wonderful! It belongs to you.' And so Smithy signed a contract and the chest was delivered a few days later." This chest, designed by former Cranbrook student Paul Evans, weighs two thousand pounds and is made with slate, steel, bronze and iron. It has four doors that weigh 200 pounds apiece that open to an interior storage area.

"When we discovered that artists were willing to sell their art on a payment plan, our art collection made great strides," Sara says. "Up until that time, we had always paid cash, but after that, we bought things on time. One artist said he would take any amount down, no matter how small it was, even five dollars, and so much a month. He said if he had ten or 12 or 15 or even 20 people sending in five or ten or fifteen dollars a month, it would add up, and if he sold that way, he could count on the money coming in so that he could maintain his home and have enough food.

"Well, when we found that out, there was no stopping us," Sara says, bursting into laughter. "From then on, we would have ten or twelve artists going at a time. When we saw a piece of art we loved at a price we couldn't handle, that's how we got it. One time, when Sam Apple was graduating from Cranbrook, he had designed a floor piece about seven feet long and two feet wide. Smithy said, 'Sam, if you would cut this piece down to my specification, I would buy it and mount it on the wall. I can't leave it on the floor because it would be a safety hazard.' Sam said there was no way he would cut this piece. And so Smithy couldn't buy it. But a few days later, Sam called Smithy and said, 'I'm packing to go back to New York and the sculpture you liked won't fit into my camper, so I will cut it down to your specification if you still want it.' So it's now in our living room."

One of the most impressive pieces they bought was a bronze sculpture by world-renowned artist, Marshall Fredricks, of a leaping gazelle, which they placed on the Paul Evans steel chest. A weaver, Barbara Wittenburg, whose work Smithy and Sara purchased, not only became a close friend, but eventually ended up making most of Sara's unique and artistic clothing. Smithy and Sara also purchased a number of other small interior pieces from the sculptor Jim Messana. And another young sculptor, Robert Scheffman from Wayne State, created a bronze bust of Smithy that today sits on the grand concert Steinway piano in the living area of the house.

"Later on, when Smithy met artists that he felt were talented, he would allow them to have a showing of their work at our house, and the artists could have all the money they earned," says Sara. "At galleries, the artists had to share up to 50 percent of the proceeds with the gallery. But at our house, besides charging the artists nothing, Smithy also would end up purchasing art from them." Smithy and Sara loved having gatherings at their home and welcomed almost any excuse—planned or unplanned—to host artists, as well as actors, friends and other visitors —for music, for singing, for acting, or just for talking, having fun, and enjoying the atmosphere.

One of the many artists Smithy happened upon was the sculptor, Mike Calligan. Calligan was a 30-year-old graduate student getting his

MFA at Cranbrook when Sara and Smithy first saw a large abstract piece he had welded from Cor-ten steel, a steel that oxidizes very rapidly to form an outer patina that hardens to protect the interior steel from structural deterioration. This steel, which is often used in bridges over expressways, has a beautiful reddish brown color and never needs painting or maintenance. The sculpture, a free-form "natural bridge," was particularly impressive because of its complex shape and the intricate welding techniques Calligan used. The moment he saw the sculpture, Smithy knew he wanted it for the grounds, and he arranged with Calligan to buy it. He thought that it fit the grounds better than anything he had ever seen, and he anticipated what a visual treat it would be at any time of the year. He might never have imagined, however, that the world-renowned architectural photographer, Balthazar Korab, would one day photograph Calligan's sculpture with their home in the background and that eventually that photograph would show up in art books and on various calendars featuring Frank Lloyd Wright's work.

"It's amazing. Smithy was so adventuresome," Sara says. "He would forge right ahead, even though it seemed like we couldn't afford it, somehow or other, we just managed. It was beautiful how those things worked out for us." Meanwhile, the interior of their house became filled with weavings, paintings, pottery, ceramics and sculpture. Outside as well, beautiful pieces of sculpture began to nestle into the artistic landscape.

Standing outside the deep-rust colored home one sunny spring afternoon, architect and professor Fred Bidigare, looks around him with a sense of wonder on his face and shakes his head. "This is a masterpiece, a little masterpiece," says Bidigare, who has had a 30-year relationship with the Smiths and their house. "It's a beautiful place to look at, a beautiful place to be at and a beautiful place to be a part of. There's more good architecture here than in 99.99 percent of any other buildings that you'll ever see. If you look at some of the things that are going on here, as an architect, you just shake your head.

"This place, besides being a great example of passive solar energy and a fantastic architectural teaching tool for students, is simply magnificent. Look at the genius of light! See how the sunlight is hitting that part of the living room, that part of the bedroom? That's all planned. At night or in the evening, and especially during the winter at night, this house looks like a Christmas tree. You see this crystal quality in these lights. There are 250 lights here, individual light bulbs, and they're all different. My favorite time of the year here is October, and the second favorite is January. At night, during a full moon, you can read inside without any lights on!

"This openness, this sense of space, was part of the design. There are no drapes. No window treatments. There can't be. In fact, Sara says that when she and Smithy used to wake up in the mornings, and during the winter especially, they'd always see rabbit tracks or squirrel or human tracks going right up to the window.

"Frank Lloyd Wright's genius shows here, but he had to have a particular client to be able to construct his ideas, to make it happen. And Smithy and Sara were the right clients. They've had an impact on a zillion lives—both of them. This place reflects the spirit of the two of them. Their spirit was so different. Smithy so intense, Sara so temperate. Yet they had the same goal. They knew what their goals were and they knew what their individual roles were.

"Smithy was the set designer. He created the set. He created the background and the stage, and he loved it. He'd sit out here on this bench looking at the house and talk. He'd say, 'Look at that wood.' He loved the wood. Loved the brick. Loved the trees. Loved the light . . .

"But this house was Sara's stage. You know she had wanted to be an actress, and here, she was the star. Smithy built it for both of them, and Smithy did most, if not all, of the selections for the scenery for this stage, but Sara was the one primarily responsible for the actors on the stage that became their home and affected so many lives.

"We all know there's something very special, very magical about this place," said Bidigare. "There's always been some magic here. The word 'dream' I don't like. But I like the word magic. There *is* an awful lot of magic. Things we don't understand. Things that are mysterious.

"To do what they did here is magical. It is. And it's still going on."

"There is no future moment, no past moment, but only this moment right now," Sara says. "The thought of knowing that this minute is the only minute I have helps me meet any challenge that might come to my mental household. For example, if someone has hurt my feelings, if I am thinking, 'This is the only minute I have—right now,' then I don't want to fill that minute with resentment. I want it filled with joy, peace, happiness and love. How could I possibly entertain one negative thought? This is the only minute you have, so make the most of it."

Chapter 17

LIGHTS, CAMERA:
The Play Goes On

FOR ALL OF SMITHY'S PURSUITS inside and outside of the house, he had Sara's full support and admiration. "I can't tell you how hard Smithy worked," she says. "He was up early and he worked late. I was not such a worker myself. I did not help him with the outside at all. I just wasn't that type. We met a girl at Taliesin who lived up in Minnesota. And this girl even mixed clay for the cement blocks they used in their home. She was a marvelous worker. But I just couldn't do that sort of physical labor, and I think Smithy understood because he never demanded that I do anything like that. I taught school and I took care of the home inside—the washing, the laundry, the cooking. But Smithy and Bobby also used to help me with those things."

Bob remembers the value of his mother's contributions. "She realized that Dad needed money," he says. "You know, they didn't make much money, and they needed somebody to work during the summer to help pay the bills. A lot of schoolteachers got second jobs. But my dad didn't want to work in the summers because he wanted to work at the house. So, Mom got a job at Cranbrook Summer Theater School, and that paid for a lot of our bills during the summer. It served Dad's purposes as well as fulfilling her needs and interests, too."

When Sara came home from teaching children at the summer theater, she helped a little around the yard and then did some household work. "We never had anybody clean the house," Bob recalls. "As I got older, that was my Saturday morning job. It would take me an hour and a half to vacuum and mop all the floors and half an hour to dust and

polish all the table tops. When I finished inside, I would sweep the terraces, and then I was free to go do my thing. That was almost every
Saturday, from sixth grade through high school. When I was younger
and I couldn't do that, I was always out helping in the garden."

It was true that as much as Sara enjoyed their Frank Lloyd Wright
home and the aesthetic and social environment it provided, it never was
her only love. Her passion was still with the stage, where she had carved
out and maintained her own special niche. As an actress, drama teacher,
director and producer of young people's theater, Sara radiated a brilliance that secured her work throughout the school years as well as during the summers. At a time many women did not work outside the
home, Sara not only taught drama ("auditorium") at school full time,
but she also was acting in plays in the local theater. For 13 years, she
directed musicals at the Cranbrook Summer Theater School. What's
more, she conducted herself through all these various activities with an
infectious sense of fun and playfulness that sprang from her joy at doing
what *she* wanted to do.

"I fell in love with Sara on the stage before I ever met her," says her
niece-by-marriage, Dorie Shwedel, who first saw Sara in *The Cocktail
Party* at St. Dunston's Theater. "On stage, Sara was very dramatic, and
I was entranced. And when I met her afterwards, she hugged and kissed
me. I was blown away by the genuine love of this family. It was so fun,
and in this family, fun was the order of the day. It wasn't a by-product.
It was the purpose."

Eventually, Dorie also saw Sara teach. "When she taught auditorium, she taught children how to be poised," says Dorie. "She gave
them confidence. And she spoke to the children with such respect and
such love. She would never discipline a child; there was no reason to.
She would tell them, 'I know that there's a treasure inside each of you,
and that you will reach in, and you will pull a little piece of it out, and
you will share it with the rest of the class. And then we'll put something
back into your little treasure house.' And her talk about treasure conjured up so much beauty and so much love. They used to follow her around like a little pied piper."

Another of Sara's habits was to meet and greet each child at the door by name. Marie Guyton, who was in the Detroit school system for 40 years and principal of the Dawson School when Sara was there, remembers the way Sara interacted with children even when she was just beginning her teaching career. "Sara was working with third graders when we got to know each other," Marie said during an interview when she was 91. "She always was a wonderful teacher, and she felt that greeting people was very important. As the children came in every morning, she shook hands with each one and said, 'Good morning! Have a wonderful day today.' She would say the same thing every day. And I thought, 'Well, now, that's kind of interesting.' She took the time to meet and greet each child and listen to something that he or she had to say to her, too. I thought, what a wonderful way to begin class. The experience helped those children gain a self-assurance to carry with them wherever they went.

"Sara had the power to influence you," said Ms. Guyton. "She would look at you and speak with you, and you understood what she wanted. And somehow you always thought it was good."

As a teacher, Sara was committed to honoring each child—and that included honoring the way they learned. One time when she was teaching fifth grade at Marsh Elementary, a girl and a boy came into Sara's class, and she discovered that neither of them could read. "Both fifth graders had entered our school in kindergarten, and the teachers just kept passing them on from one grade to the next." Sara recalls. "If I complained, then the teachers would have been blamed. So, what I did was this: we had extra time to read from 11 to 11:30, so I had these two kids on either side of me. So I got out *Robinson Crusoe* and *Huckleberry Finn* and other exciting stories. I read, and they sat there and listened; they were interested in what came next. I had two brilliant students sitting on each side of those two, and so they would point to words they didn't know and the other two would tell them the words. By the time we finished a couple of those books, they had started reading. Both of them became fine readers."

No matter where Sara is, children gather around her, says Sophie Plopa, a friend of Sara's for 37 years. "We'd go some place, and if children were there, Sara was like a magnet. There'd be everybody else, but Sara was with the children, telling them stories. They'd sit around her and they'd listen. She is so giving with everybody, but especially with children."

St. Dunston's Theater, which has framed montages of various plays, is a good place to see pictures of Sara. "Sara's picture is in at least a dozen or more of the montages," says Marvin Shwedel. "She either directed the play or acted in it. I think her ability to put her philosophy to work in the theater has had a profound impact on many lives."

Sara often uses examples from plays she has acted in to make a point or to teach a lesson. For instance, she tells how, in Thornton Wilder's play, *Our Town*, Emily dies at childbirth, but just after her death, she has one request. "She wants to visit one day of her life in her home," Sara says. "Of course her family could not see her, but she could see them and talk to them. When the day ends and Emily is ready to leave the world, never to return, she says, *'Oh Earth, you are too wonderful for anybody to realize you. Do any human beings ever realize life while they live it? Every minute—every minute.'*

"We have to know that this minute is the only minute we have," Sara continues. "There is no future moment, no past moment, but only this moment right now. The thought of knowing that this minute is the only minute I have helps me meet any challenge that might come to my mental household. For example, if someone has hurt my feelings, if I am thinking, 'This is the only minute I have, right now,' then I don't want to fill that minute with resentment. I want it filed with joy from peace, happiness and love. How could I possibly entertain one negative thought? This is the only minute you have, so make the most of it."

Sara's skills at nurturing were not only exhibited on stage or in her relationships with those she was teaching. They also were woven into her friendships with family and friends. Her talent for friendship is legendary, and nowhere did it shine with a more intense light than it did with her sister Thelma, who always was her best friend. Family members recall that it was as if they'd been born out of the same egg; they were in perfect harmony with one another.

When Nathan Stein died, and later, when Annie Stein died, it was sad for all the Stein sisters, but Thelma took it the hardest. "My mom went through an extremely hard time and ended up in the hospital," says Marvin. "But about eight months before my bar mitzvah, she got better, and my father told me that the reason that she got well was Aunt Sara. My Aunt Sara went to see her every single day at the hospital and she'd talk. It took a long time, but she talked my mother through it and got her out of her depression. Sara basically healed her and enabled her to become a functioning human being for the rest of her life.

"Sara always was my mother's lifeline. And, interestingly enough, my mother became the lifeline for other people, and sort of carried on what she had learned from Sara. She got the ability to find the good in life, as opposed to finding what's wrong—it's easy to find what's wrong. I would say that my mother learned what was valuable and important from my Aunt Sara through this intense relationship with her, and then she continued to do the same thing for other people.

"I know of other instances where my Aunt Sara has given people hope and the ability to see the good side of the situation instead of the bad side. She loves helping people find the ability to cope with their problems. She never wants to get even or take advantage of another human being. She always brings out the best in others; that's one of her greatest strengths. It's just amazing. I've learned so much in that regard from her. She's really the hero among a lot of people for her attitude toward life and her ability to bring out the best in them, even when they're not necessarily going to have her best interest at heart. That's unique. She only looks for the good in everybody. I've never heard her make a criticism about anybody in her whole life."

If anything, Sara has always been an advocate and safe haven for anyone who has been injured by other people's criticisms. She remembers one boy who was captain of the school crossing patrol. "He came up to me one day and said, 'I'm a weirdo,'" she recalls. I told him, 'No, you're not.' He said, 'Yes, I am.' I said, 'Now look. Every boy would love to be able do what you're doing. You've just got to be proud of yourself every day. Be kind to yourself every day.' He said, 'Well, I'll try. I'll try.'"

When a visitor speculates that that boy—now a man—probably still tells people about his fifth grade teacher who taught him to feel good about himself, Sara smiles and shrugs. "Well, you have to help children. That's what we're here for. It's that simple."

"When Smithy had an idea, there wasn't anything that would stop him," says Sara. "The minute you have an idea, don't say, 'Oh, it's impossible.' Know that it's possible! If you nurture the idea, you'll get more ideas that will take care of the first idea—and it will expand from there. To expand is to progress—and life can become all that much more interesting!"

Chapter 18

SHIFTING PATTERNS
OF LIFE

In 1978, BOB SMITH FLEW IN FROM WASHINGTON, D.C., where he was working as Assistant Director of the Community Services Administration for President Carter, to attend his father's retirement celebration. While Smithy and Sara had been enjoying a slower pace, Bob's life had been gaining a momentum of its own. After graduating from Bloomfield Hills High School, where he was president of his sophomore class, yearbook editor, and a member of the student government council, Bob had gone on to graduate from the University of Michigan in 1967 and from the University of Michigan Law School in 1970.

Before President Jimmy Carter selected him for his presidential appointment in 1977, Bob had worked as an attorney for the Federal Communications Commission. Then he had become Director of Youth Affairs for the Democratic National Committee and National Coordinator of the Democratic National Committee's Voter Registration/Get Out the Vote campaign for the 1976 presidential elections. The day after President Carter's inauguration ceremony, he became a member of the Carter White House Staff. He held that job until he was nominated by President Carter to become Assistant Director of the Community Services Administration, where he was responsible for many of the poverty programs administered by the original Office of Economic Opportunity in the mid 1960s. As assistant director of that agency, he was one of the leading administrators of poverty programs in this country.

Bob felt that because of the values his father had taught him, he had done things he otherwise might never have attempted. "When I first went to Washington, I said, 'Well, someday I'm going to be working in the White House,'" Bob says. "People would say, 'Forget it, everybody wants to work in the White House.' But I had my father's example; I had that self-determination, that drive that said, 'I don't care what anybody says. I can achieve my goals against all odds if I put my mind to it.'"

Bob was remembering those lessons as he watched the retirement ceremonies honoring his father. He listened with awe as the students at Cody High School said their farewells. Smithy had taught in the Detroit public school system for 38 years, and he had absolutely loved his job. He had always said that if he could influence one person's life through his teaching, if he could help one person have a better understanding of life, then he could consider himself a success. Clearly, he had gone far beyond that goal. "When he said goodbye to his class," Bob remembers, "it was very emotional. Some of his former students had come back for this event, and all of them gave him a standing ovation. He was basically like the teacher in the *Dead Poets' Society*. He just sort of threw the books away and taught people from his heart. He challenged his students to think outside the box. He used great authors to teach his students great ideas about life—ideas that would affect them as long as they lived."

As he watched his father, Bob thought about how he appreciated him, even though his dad sometimes had been hard on him. For although Smithy was tremendously proud of Bob, he also had been a tough and demanding critic. It was at his insistence, for instance, that Bob had become an Eagle Scout—a goal that had been of primary importance to Smithy because being an Eagle Scout had so shaped his own life. But it was much less important to Bob. "We got into vicious fights because he would drive me and drive me so hard," says Bob. "As a result, I became an Eagle Scout in record time. One summer, he pushed me to get 13 merit badges, and that meant working morning, noon, night, and all weekend long. Eventually I earned 36 merit badges, but you only needed 21 to become an Eagle Scout. Initially, I resented it, and then later, I appreciated it. Overall, I'm happy I got it for him, and I'm happy I got it for myself, but it was just one of those things that *he* passionately wanted to achieve."

Smithy had also always demanded precision on Bob's part in keeping the house and grounds in as perfect a condition as possible. Furniture in the house had to be *exactly* positioned, and work on the yard had to be thorough and carried out to Smithy's precise instructions. Bob and Sara both recall Smithy's standards of perfection in the garden. Both Bob and his mother laugh at the memory of the time when Smithy, furious and disgusted with their performances as gardeners, fired them both—as in, *You're fired!*—a dismissal that they didn't mind in the least, and in fact welcomed with a shared but discreet hilarity.

"Ironically, he never pressured me on academics," says Bob. "I was street smart, but I was never an A student. I was basically a C+/B- student, which was not an issue to him. He never came home and said 'Why aren't you getting A's?' He would always say, 'Get enough good grades, get into school, and become a teacher—they can't fire teachers. Or, become a doctor or an attorney.'"

Of course Smithy had been very happy when Bob decided to go to law school. "He said, 'You will always have a profession,'" Bob says. "Business was something he was scared to death of because he thought if you go into business, and if they don't want you, they could fire you. He'd say, 'There's no security in business.' He was always concerned about being able to retire with a pension. Actually, he would have been terrific in business, but he just didn't trust it because he had seen too many people hurt by the Depression.

"But down deep, he was a tremendous cheerleader. He was very proud. I changed my career three or four times, and when I entered politics, he may have been worried about my security. But he was always there for me. He helped me financially whenever I needed it, even though he didn't have much. He was a very generous man and such a loving person. Sometimes he was just very difficult because once he thought he was right, he was right."

Despite Smithy's stubbornness, despite his demands, and perhaps in large part because of them, Bob came to believe that he, too, could make his dreams come true. He trusted his own instincts, and like both his mother and his father, he had a charisma that made him an effective organizer and leader. He had seen both of his parents take risks, face hurdles and jump over them, and he learned to do the same. In 1962, for instance, when Bob was a senior in high school and yearbook editor, he created a highly unusual and controversial cover for the high school yearbook with a photograph of construction pipes. One detractor had said, "How can you put sewer pipes on the cover of our yearbook?!" But the school had been under construction all year, so it made sense to Bob for the front of the yearbook to be a photograph of the construction piles all put together in a geometric pattern. He thought it was artistic, that it created a mood and told a story, and so he did it.

"I had learned from my dad," Bob says, "and when I was yearbook editor, I would go back to his yearbook—*The Cody Comet*—and take ideas from his layouts. He was so artistic, and he would just tell the story of what happened during the year. He would always create a mood and an atmosphere. So when I was editor, I tried to create the same feeling. I wrote poetry for the whole thing and tied it all together with pictures. We ended up winning the same national award that he had won."

Bob says that in addition to teaching him an early love of the outdoors, his dad also taught him about the values of human rights. "He taught me at a very young age about the civil rights movement, about treating people equally, and making a commitment to work for racial equality," says Bob. "He would always say that we have been provided a lot of the blessings of life, and it's our obligation to give back and help the people who are disadvantaged. He always believed that working for racial equality was one of the most important things you could do in life. As a result of growing up with that philosophy, I became very much involved in the political movement in the 1960s, both in high school and college.

"Through my dad, I was exposed to a person who was willing to sacrifice things for himself to achieve his goals. He'd always figure out a way to get things done." Like both of his parents, Bob was blessed with spontaneity and tenacity. He was the one, for instance, who set up the White House meetings with the president of Chrysler that would eventually lead to the bailout of the Chrysler Corporation. This happened because one day Bob saw John Ricardo, chairman of the board and president of Chrysler, sitting in the lobby of the west wing of the White House. "I knew John because I had been an intern at Chrysler during law school," Bob says. "I went up and asked him what he was doing there, and he said he was trying to get an appointment to talk to some-body about the awful financial condition of Chrysler Corporation. But he was having a hard time finding someone at the White House to meet with him. He said, 'We're having a tough time surviving.'

"I went to talk to Hamilton Jordan, who was President Carter's Chief of Staff, and Jordan said, 'Well, you're from Detroit. You take care of the problem.' So I went back to John Ricardo and said, 'How can I help?' He said, 'Get me to somebody.' So I set up an appointment later that afternoon for him to meet with Stuart Eisenstadt to discuss the Chrysler problem. Soon after that, Lee Iacocca replaced Ricardo as president of Chrysler, and the discussions with Eisenstadt continued. The rest—how Iacocco succeeded in negotiating the successful Chrysler bailout plan—is history."

Later in life Bob would go on to tackle other difficult tasks in the business world—becoming the president and majority stockholder of Smith Broadcasting Group and owning controlling interests in more than ten television stations and having a minority ownership interest in another sixteen.

One of the most extraordinary and improbable undertakings of his life, however, was the seven-year campaign he conducted, beginning in the mid-1960s, to woo and win a young woman named Anne Fuchs, who had no interest whatsoever in becoming romantically involved with him. Given Anne's attitude at the time, some observers might have thought Bob's prospects with the petite, dark-haired dynamo were per-haps even more unlikely than the dream of a Frank Lloyd Wright house had been for Smithy.

The way Anne tells it, she was a senior in high school and Bob was a junior at the University of Michigan when her sister Suzy, who was working on a winter weekend event committee with Bob, introduced them in 1965. "He was a perfect gentleman, but he thought he was going to sweep me off my feet," Anne says. "He figured he was a big col-lege guy, I was a high school kid, I'd be head over heels for him. We went out and had a good time at the University of Michigan on our first date, but then a couple of weeks later he came down to visit me. As I got into the car to go to the movie, I put my hand out and said, 'I just want you to get one thing straight. I'd like to be friends, but that's all. You're not my type. If you don't want to take me out as a friend, that's fine. I'll understand.'

"I was pretty discouraging to him. But we did go out, and we had a great time, and over the next five years, we were just friends. I would just never kiss him. He would call me and I would call him, and I would tell him all the things happening in my life, and he would do the same. We were confidants, but I just had this thing about not getting physically involved with him. Some nights we would go out for dinner or a movie, and then Bob would go back to his apartment and want to put his fist through the wall. His roommate, Chuck West, would say, 'No action tonight? Did you get dumped on again?' I went through four years of college and dated the NCAA wrestling champion and a number of other guys. And then, after I graduated, I went on a trip around the world. Right before I left, I told Bob not to wait for me, that he was a great guy, and that he should find a woman who would appreciate him.

"Before I left on this year-long trip, I had been seriously dating a tall, blond and real handsome guy named Gary, who had played golf for Michigan. He broke up with me to date a girl named Carolyn, and when I was away, I heard that Carolyn had left Gary for Bob. I remember thinking about it and wondering, how could Carolyn dump such a sexy guy like Gary for Bob? By the time I got back, Bob and Carolyn had stopped dating because of the pressures her family had put on her for dating a Jewish guy. I had gone back to Ann Arbor to start my master's degree and Bob was there in law school. I remember looking at him, and I still couldn't get excited about him. He said, 'Well, maybe I'm not the kind of guy you can date. But since you need a place to live during the summer while you start your master's degree, and I'm here getting my law degree, why don't we live together?'

"Well, I just laughed. And I remember going to the theater with my sister and telling her what Bob said and laughing about it with her. Can you believe that? Bob kept saying, 'You're afraid to make yourself vulnerable to me. If you would open yourself up, you might learn to love me.' I'd say, 'You've got to be kidding.' I was mean. One time he hurt his knee coming over to play tennis with me, and I wouldn't even go to the hospital to visit because I didn't want him to think I cared for him.

"Soon after that conversation about living together, he invited me to a wedding. I remember, we were driving home from the wedding past Ralph's Market, and he stopped the car and said, 'You know, I've just had a real meaningful romance with Carolyn. It was fantastic—bells and whistles—and so I know what a relationship can be. I want you to know you're the coldest bitch in the world. I have been a gentleman for six years, and you won't even let me kiss you. You are afraid of me, afraid of commitment, and afraid to lose our friendship. I'm here to tell you, I don't want to be your friend any more. If you don't give me a chance romantically, I never want to see you again under any circumstances.'

"We're right in front of Ralph's Market. A voice came through me—I had no control over this voice—and it said 'Let's live together.' I truly had no control over that voice. I can hear it to this day. We were sitting in the car, and those incredible words just came through me. I thought to myself, 'Well, maybe he's *not* the kind of guy that I would date, but maybe he is the kind of guy I could live with.'

"My parents were happy Bob and I would share an apartment during the summer. After all, they knew I would never fall in love with Bob, and it was safer for me to room with him than to be alone in an apartment."

But Bob's campaign was just gathering steam. "We did get a place," Anne says. "However, I had my conditions. I said, 'Hey, I'll room with you, but I'm still going to date,' and so Bob said, 'That's fine.' He knew that anybody in their right mind could only take it so long. At the time I was dating a tall blond doctor. I'd go out with him, and then I'd come home, and there would be this guy in the apartment. So, Bob waited it out a few weeks, and sure enough, the doctor fell by the wayside, and I had to face my demons.

"I was keeping a journal every night, and I was locking the door, shutting him out. One day he had had enough, and he began banging on the door, saying, 'Talk to me. Don't talk to that journal, talk to me. Tell me what you're thinking. Tell me what's inside your heart.' Finally, that night, he would not take no for an answer. He broke the door down. I started crying and talking to him, and slowly the walls tumbled. I realized he was such a good person. And now, you know, I think he's perfect for me. As the years go by, he ages like fine wine."

When Bob and Anne got married in September, 1971, they wrote a poem, "Before We Were One," for their wedding ceremony that reflected the separate paths they had taken.

Before we were one we were two.
Everyday belongs to each of us.
We both laughed at different things
*　　and smiled at different people*
*　　and walked on different paths*
*　　and ran on separate sea shores.*

Before we were one we were two.
Busy with our own blueprints
*　　and firm foundations*
*　　and bright decorations*
*　　and fitting into the scenery.*

Because we were two, we can find joy in being one.
Our different pasts now fuse to enrich the whole.
And all the times we skipped stones separately
*　　make all sense now.*

They began a marriage that not only flourished, but that also gave Sara and Smithy the daughter they had wanted for a long time. When Bob was still young, Smithy had told Sara he wanted to have another child, specifically a daughter, and Sara had responded, "When Bobby gets married, then you'll have your daughter." For both Sara and Smithy, Anne, a dynamic, energetic and beautiful girl with an enormous smile, was a dream come true.

"To this day, Bob wonders why he didn't give up on me earlier," Anne says. "But Sara had always told him, 'If it's meant to be, it will happen. There is only the one plan, and that's God's plan. You need to put your trust in God. If she's the right person for you, nobody can take her away.'"

For Sara, of course, Anne was the *perfect* daughter-in-law, and she helped Anne to feel "absolutely embraced by this family." An added bonus was that many of Anne's interests coincided with Sara's. From the time she was small, Anne, too, had been an actress. In the all-girls camp she went to as a child, Anne always played the male lead because she had a beautiful singing voice that also happened to be the lowest voice in camp. She was Billy Bigelow in *Carousel* and Professor Harold Hill in *The Music Man*. She had acted in plays up until her second year in college, when she realized she liked directing much better.

Besides her commitment to theater, which would last all of her life, Anne also loved literature and teaching. At the University of Michigan, she had majored in English, and when she got her master's degree, it was in English and education. When she and Bob moved to Maryland, Anne, a charismatic and creative teacher, taught drama and English in high school. Since Anne also was a singer, she used a lot of music in her teaching. With young language arts students, for instance, she'd *sing* the parts of speech, and they would sing with her: *A noun names a person, place or thing — like love, power, book, and a ring.*

"They'd learn the songs," Anne says, "and when they came to tests or whatever, you'd hear all this humming going on. I enjoyed teaching, and I loved the theater, so I guess I was like Sara in that way. I always loved Sara, and I learned so much from her. I learned a great deal from seeing her direct, and she also gave me a lot of scripts to work with.

"Besides teaching me a lot about the theater, she also has made me a more open, loving person. I never hugged people before. I came from a caring family, but we were not as demonstrative as they are. Now I hug everybody—it's absolutely habit. There are some times it's not appropriate, you know, like hugging the waitress. So I try to control myself, but it seems very formal to me to shake someone's hand. I think it's important to touch people in some way to make a connection.

"Sara also has taught me the art of small talk, which is to ask other people about themselves, to get them talking. When you ask the questions, it's easy to have conversations because people love to talk about themselves."

When Smithy retired from teaching, Sara also retired, but she continued to act and direct at St. Dunstan's Community Playhouse. And although Bob and Anne lived in Maryland, they talked on the phone every night with Smithy and Sara. When Michigan football games were being played, Smithy would call Bob every 30 minutes with the score, no matter where Bob was. And when Sara wasn't in the middle of directing a play, or when they weren't hosting an artist's exhibition or a concert at their home, Smithy and Sara often traveled to Columbia, Maryland to see Bob and Anne and now also their two treasured grandchildren, Jennifer and Michael, who were born in 1975 and 1977 respectively.

Today Jennifer, who graduated from Pepperdine University in Malibu in 1997, still lights up at the memories of her grandmother and grandfather coming to Columbia. "I remember when I was really young—like three or four years old," says Jennifer, "and I used to lie on the bed backwards, and she would tell me a story. But her chin and her mouth backwards would look like a nose and a mouth upside down, and she used to tell these funny stories, and I would watch her whole face move. It was fun. I loved that. I'd say, 'Do it again!' And she used to tell great bedtime stories. She was wonderful at that. She'd make them up right then and there.

"She also made great marshmallow treats by dripping her special hot fudge sauce all over the marshmallows. When my grandma and grandpa visited, we'd always get to stay up late, and talk, and play hide-and-go-seek. It was wonderful."

On their visits to Maryland, Sara and Smithy also had the experience of going to the White House while Bob was on staff. Meeting the President of the United States was an event both Sara and Smithy found thrilling, but they took it into stride. Like everything else, it seemed like one of life's miracles—a surprise not so surprising after all.

Sara says, "Promise yourself to be strong so that nothing can disturb your peace of mind."

Chapter 19

NEW DREAMS AND
HORIZONS

Rᴇᴛɪʀᴇᴍᴇɴᴛ ʙʀᴏᴜɢʜᴛ ɴᴇᴡ ᴏᴘᴘᴏʀᴛᴜɴɪᴛɪᴇꜱ and adventures to both
Smithy and Sara. Smithy had always remained grateful to Jane Betsy
Welling, the humanities professor who had introduced him to Frank
Lloyd Wright, and to Wayne State University, where he had learned so
much that contributed to his life. He stayed active in Wayne State alumni
activities, and in the mid-1970s, he worked on a committee whose goal
was to bring focus to the Visual Arts program at Wayne State. The committee mounted two arts festivals on campus, and Smithy was instru-
mental in bringing many of the artists he had come to know to the campus.

Wayne State professor Richard Belitus, who also worked on the
committee, remembers mentioning very briefly at one of the meetings
that someday he hoped to have a small sculpture court near the art
wing—an outdoor setting where sculpture done by students could be
temporarily moored, not permanently installed. His thought was to
show student art that might otherwise never be seen by the public. The
temporary exhibits would be a boost for the student artists who would
have a chance to see their art viewed in compatible surroundings, rather
than just in studio workshops. And the sculpture court, in his opinion,
was a perfect location for the art. "As I talked about it, I could see
Smithy's excitement mounting," Professor Belitus later recalled. "Two
years later, through his and Sara's support, we dedicated that court to
Jane Betsy Welling; it's the Jane Betsy Welling Sculpture Court. Sara and
Smithy were the major donors, and they brought along with them
countless art alumni and others who supported the project, which is

right outside the art wing, and something I see daily and enjoy all the time. The Smiths have been most generous to us, most generous to Cranbrook, and generous to art in general."

Smithy's patronage of the arts and support of local artists had enriched their life on many levels. In addition to the pleasure of seeing young artists succeed, he loved being able to buy their art for his and Sara's home. On the grounds outside of their home, they now had four steel pieces of sculpture by Cranbrook artist Michael Calligan. Along with the first and largest sculpture, the free form "natural bridge," another large sculpture also has been photographed extensively and is a favorite of Sara's: six standing geometric forms that she refers to as her "marching soldiers." When the cypress on the exterior of the house became slightly discolored over the years and warped in certain places, Sara and Smithy were able to hire Calligan to apply his skills to restoring the wood. Under Smithy's intense supervision, Calligan sanded it and finished it with oil, which restored its healthy sheen.

For the first time, in the late 70's and 80's, Sara and Smithy were able to take advantage of the many invitations they had to visit friends in Florida and California. A particularly special trip was one they made to Scottsdale, Arizona, where they visited Frank Lloyd Wright's second home, Taliesin West, and talked with many of the architects who had been his students there. Those students all knew the story of Wright's "little gem" in Bloomfield Hills, Michigan. They knew that, even to Wright, it was a magical place and was still one of the finest examples of his Usonian period. The fact that the house had been judged by the American Institute of Architecture (AIA) as one of the most beautiful structures in the six-county area of Southeastern Michigan, had added to its status and was bringing even more visitors to the door than before. Although it was a low-maintenance house, Smithy, of course, still maintained it to perfection. Thirty-one years after it was built, it still gave them just as much pleasure, if not more so, than when they first occupied it.

Adding to the spontaneity of their retirement years was the fact that in 1980, Bob and Anne decided to move back to Michigan to be closer to their families. Bob decided to go into consulting and television broadcasting. Anne taught fourth and fifth grades at Brookside School, part of the Cranbrook educational community, where eventually she would have both Jennifer and Michael in her class. Smithy and Sara were thrilled to have Bob and Anne and their grandchildren so geographically close. And for the grandchildren, it was a bonanza. Jennifer, who was five when they moved back to Michigan, remembers her stays at My Haven. "After Grandpa retired, he liked to watch 'The Young and the Restless' on television," Jennifer says. "It was so different from what he was really like, but he was into the soaps. We would sit there with our little trays in front of the TV—my grandma, my grandfather, and me—and we would have lunch and watch the soaps. It was really fun."

Michael also remembers going over to his grandparents' house a lot. "The house was always kind of a magical place," he recalls. "My dad put it in such a context that it really stood out in my mind. And so, whenever I was there playing with the ducks by the lake, or outside on the patio eating Grandma's cookies, it was something special, and I knew that from the beginning. Grandma really made me feel amazing in that place. My earliest memories of her, funny enough, were actually in the kitchen. Grandpa would be outside, and she'd be hard at work, making treats in the kitchen. She's always loved to make people happy."

Smithy, with his baseball cap on his head, loved driving his tractor-mower around the property with his grandchildren and grandnieces and nephews clinging to his shoulders and squealing with delight. Michael remembers many such crowded rides, as well as the times he rode solo with his grandpa. "One time when I was four or five, he took me for a tractor ride, and the tractor broke down," Michael says. "We rolled down a hill, all the way back to the house. And my grandma thought that was just the funniest thing. I said 'trakta, trakta,' and she loved it.

"We came in, and we had dinner, and that same night, we went camping, my grandpa and me. He had put up this hammock outside between two big oak trees, and we were going to sleep there, but for some reason it broke. It kind of collapsed and wrapped me and my grandpa in this little pea pod kind of thing. We were trapped in there, trying to get out. He was pretty frustrated, saying, 'I can't do a tent right!' But he was laughing, too. He wanted to get everything perfect, but at the same time, he laughed it off with me, and we had fun. We came inside and slept on mats on the floor. It was so funny. It was an unbelievable day. And he was amazing. Unfortunately, I never really knew him as well as I would have liked to, because I lost him when I was seven."

Besides wanting Michael and Jennifer to be able to spend more time with their grandparents, one of the reasons that Bob had been particularly eager to move back to Michigan was his concern about his dad's health. With both of his parents seeming more vulnerable, he wanted to be available to check in on them every day.

Bob's worries about his parents had begun when he was a junior in high school and his seemingly invincible 49-year-old father had a heart attack. It happened when Smithy was climbing the stairs at school. Sara and Bob had gotten a call telling them that he had been taken by ambulance to the hospital. The attack was frightening, but Smithy lived through it and spent three weeks in the hospital—which was the longest period that he and Sara had ever been separated.

During Bob's senior year, he was reminded again of how mortal both of his parents were. At home one afternoon, he waited and waited, but neither his mother nor father arrived. "I was wondering where they were when all of a sudden, I see an ambulance come up," Bob says. "They pull Mom out of the back because she wouldn't go to the hospital. She was in a car accident, and she was hurt, but she had refused medical aid. She had said, 'I demand to go home.' So they brought my mom in on a stretcher, all bandaged up. And I was very upset, and I started praying with my mom, wondering where my dad is.

"And then I got a call from a police officer saying that Dad had been in a very bad accident. Now I was beside myself. So I called our family friends, the Afflecks, who came right over to get me. And Mrs. Affleck stayed with my mom, and Mr. Affleck took me to see my dad, who was in the hospital. Initially, I was scared to death that he was going to die.

"I couldn't believe it. What are the odds that both of them would have car accidents that same afternoon?" Bob asks. "I don't know for sure, but I think Dad might have fallen asleep at the wheel because he was very tired. He would work late at school and then he would come home and work outside. This was when he was working on the yearbook, and I think at that point it was too much. After that, he decided to give up the yearbook."

Another time, when Smithy and Sara were visiting Bob and Anne at their townhouse in Maryland, Sara was walking down the stairs when she tripped and fell two flights down to the bottom of the stairs. "It was an awful sound," Bob remembers, "and we all ran over to her. She was lying on the ground, entirely conscious, and she goes into this trance and says, 'Let me just pray, let me just pray.' I'm saying, 'Can you move, Mom? Should I call an ambulance? You could have broken bones.' She says, 'No, don't call. Just let me stay here.' After an hour or two, she said, 'You can help me up. I need help. Just set me in this chair.' So we did it. And she stayed in the chair for a few hours and prayed. We gave her *Science and Health* book to her, and she talked to a practitioner on the phone. She couldn't move. But by that evening, she got up and walked. I'm convinced that she had fractured her back. It was just unbelievable to observe her strength and determination."

Then in 1975, the year Jennifer was born, Smithy had called Bob and said he was worried about Sara; she wasn't looking well. Sara still wouldn't see a doctor or go to a hospital since she believed illness was only an illusion. "Sometimes my dad became very angry because she wouldn't seek treatment when she was sick," says Bob. "He couldn't deal with it because if he was sick, he would run to a doctor, and she wouldn't. So, he would call me."

This time, when Smithy reported that Sara seemed very sick, Bob asked him what he meant.

"I don't know," Smithy said, "but she's very lethargic and she has pains in her stomach."

"A couple days later, Dad called and said, 'Mom's getting worse. She hasn't gone to the bathroom. She's getting bloated in her stomach. Something's really wrong.' When I heard that, I rushed to Michigan and convinced my mom to travel back to Maryland with me. She was in a great deal of pain. She would try to talk to me, and then all of a sudden her eyes would go up in her head and she would fall back. She was almost in a coma. She hadn't gone to the bathroom for almost a week, and her stomach was blowing up. Dad was getting more and more upset because he was so scared. So, I said, 'Mom, you gotta see a doctor.'"

"She said, 'Bob, I can't go to the doctor. If this is the end, I can handle it. I will put my trust in God.' I said, 'But Mom, if you can't fix the problem in the short term, I think your philosophy would agree that you should try and find a temporary measure to fix the problem and then go back to your philosophy for the long term.' Later she found out this was okay, but at that time she didn't believe it.

"I knew some doctors, and I asked them to come over and look at her. I had asked them to come by on an informal basis and let me know what they thought from observing her. Just from looking, they said she was in very very bad shape. But without examining her, they didn't know what it was. There was no way they could do anything without getting an upper and lower GI. I knew my time was running out, and I said, "Look, Mom, let me just get an exam for you. Just let a doctor give you an exam. That's all I'm asking." She agreed to it because it didn't involve taking medicine.

A doctor then gave her an upper and lower GI and called me in. He said, "She's got a tumor that's probably cancerous. It's causing a large blockage in her intestine, and I predict she has at most three to four days to live if she doesn't get this operated on." I cannot tell you the feeling that went over me. I took her home, and I explained this to her. I said, 'Mom, you've got to let me do this.'

"She said, 'I can't.'

"I said, 'Mom, don't you want to see your granddaughter?'

"She said, 'Yes, but not if it means I have to have surgery.'

"I said, 'Mom, please think about it. Do you ever want to see your grandchildren? They will need you in their lives. I need you in my life. I need your prayers to get through all these things I'm doing. Everyone needs you. You just can't sit here and allow this to occur.'

"She said, 'Let me just pray.' She believed there was no question that God would resolve the problem. At that point, I said, 'Give me a *Christian Science Monitor*' because all of the practitioners in the country were listed in the back of it. I started calling every practitioner in the

Washington, Virginia, and Maryland area to explain my plight, and to find the one practitioner who would tell her that she could go and get temporary medical help and it would not be the end of her religious beliefs. Finally, on the second day of calling, I found one.

"I remember crying on the phone to this woman, describing my mom's condition and my feelings, and she said 'I'll talk to her.' I said, 'What do you mean?' She said, 'If it were only her, I would not tell her what I'm about to tell her. But because it is so important to you and your family, and because I think it would affect your life, and you would not be able to cope with it, that's not fair to you.' And she said, 'Your mom can handle this situation; that's not a problem. *You* cannot handle it.' And she said, 'I don't think what I'm telling her is wrong. I think it is right for this special situation. Put her on the phone.'

"So, I put her on the phone, and I can't tell you how many times Mom talked to her during that whole day. But they talked hour after hour, and finally Mom said, 'Okay, I'll go and I'll get the operation.'

"When we went in for her operation, there was this phenomenal surgeon named Dr. Jean-Jacques who saw her. She said to him, 'I'll take surgery, but I don't want any anesthetics.' And Dr. Jean-Jacques said, 'Pardon me?!'

"Mom said, 'I'll let you operate on me. I can allow that, but I don't want anything injected into me.'

"'Well, we can't do that,' Dr. Jean-Jacques said. 'I can't open you up and take out part of your intestine without an anesthetic.'

"'Oh yes, you can,' she says. 'I get root canals, and I don't take anything for root canals. You must understand: There's no such thing as pain. Pain is in the mind.'

"'It's not you, it's me,' Dr. Jean-Jacques said. 'I couldn't handle it.'

"So, after we went around and around, I finally said, 'Mom, if you're going to do it anyway, let's do it his way,'" Bob recounts. "'He's not as strong as you are.' Mom's sister, Thelma, flew in and she was there through the entire surgery. The night before, we sat down with the Bible, and I read her hour after hour from the Bible and *Science and Health* about healing. All during the operation, Thelma and I sat in the waiting room reading the Bible.

"After the surgery, when the doctor came out, he said, 'She's fine. We got the tumor out, and it looks as if the cancer was contained within the intestine.' Dr. Jean-Jacques was one of the finest doctors I've ever met. He understood my mom's philosophy. He was very kind and considerate of her beliefs. And I stayed every day and night with her. I wouldn't leave the hospital until I could take her home. About a day after surgery, they had to give her a blood transfusion. Every other time they put up a bag on the IV pole, we told her it was just water. But with the blood transfusion, she said, 'What's that?'

"I told her it was a blood transfusion, and it was okay. But then I was sitting there, and Mom says, 'I don't really feel well, Bobby. I don't feel well.' I said, 'Mom, the doctor said you're fine. Everything's perfect.' She says, 'I know, but something's going on and something's not right.' So, I said, 'Don't worry about it.' I called in her nurse. And the nurse checked her and said everything was fine.

"About five minutes later, Mom said, 'Bobby, I am not doing well,' and then basically her eyes started to go back into her head. She went into shock. I ran out and I yelled for a nurse. Unbelievably, Dr. Jean-Jacques was walking down the hallway—he was doing his rounds—and he saw me and came running in. He said, 'What's the matter?' I said, 'Look at Mom.' He said, 'Oh my God.' She had turned white, and her eyes had started to gloss over. Then he looked at the blood, and he said, 'Who the hell did this?' He turned off the blood and pulled the tubing off the needle. Then he shoved the IV pole with the bag of blood against the wall. He told the nurse to bring him an antidote immediately, and he started injecting it into her to counteract what was happening.

"They had given her the wrong blood type! And she was going into shock. Had I not been there, she could have been dead within just a few minutes—and after having gone through the whole thing! Dr. Jean-Jacques said to Mom, "I can't tell you that medicine is perfect. And, in fact, when I see things like this it makes me sick."

"He said, 'There was no excuse for this. All I can do is apologize.' He told my mom, 'Somehow, between your prayers and my medical techniques, we're going to get through this.'

"I said, 'Now you know why I won't leave.'"

Dr. Jean-Jacques said, "I don't want you to leave her until you get her out of this place."

So, a few days later, when Sara was better, Bob took her home. Within a few weeks, Sara returned to full strength.

It wasn't that long, however, before Smithy started slowing down, and often, he seemed quite fatigued. One afternoon in 1981, he began to have pains in his chest. "I went in with him to see the doctor," Bob remembers, "and the doctor said, 'I think he's had a mild heart attack. Let's put him in the hospital to do some tests.'"

The tests established that Smithy needed bypass surgery immediately. And because the rates of success were so positive, he readily agreed to it. His doctor suggested that he go to Milwaukee to be operated on by one of the foremost heart surgeons in the country—Dr. Dudley Johnson, who was known as "the doctor of last resort" because he would take on patients that few other doctors would attempt to cure.

At that time, Bob was doing consulting work, but he took a leave of absence so that he could be with his dad at Sinai Hospital in Milwaukee. "I wanted to be by his side every day in the hospital," says Bob. "My view is that from the moment my dad or my mom or any member of my family walks into a hospital, I'm with them until I bring them out—whether it's one day, one week or one month. And I stay with them, I sleep by their side, and I watch the nurses, and I watch everything they do. That experience with Mom confirmed how important it is to be there until you know they are out of danger. A lot of medicine is common sense. And the more I'm thinking about how to help them recover, the better it is."

Smithy had seven bypasses during a long and difficult surgery. During the following 24 hours, he struggled to survive. Bob was given special permission to be with his dad in the recovery room that first night. "I prayed constantly as I watched the person in the bed next to Dad's lose his struggle," he remembers. "But Dad slowly started to gain his strength." Bob left his father's side only to give his mother updates and to say prayers with her. But about 48 hours after the surgery, Smithy's heart went into fibrillation. The doctors made a decision to shock his heart in order to get it back into the proper rhythm.

The doctors told Bob it was a make it or break it situation. Bob told Sara, "Mom, pray like you never prayed before." Fortunately, the shock to the heart worked, and Smithy survived that life-threatening moment. Bob continued to stay with Smithy, advocate on his behalf and monitor his white blood count. When it was too low, Bob would tell the doctors that Smithy was losing blood and the doctors would give him a transfusion. All in all, he made sure that his father had the best possible medical treatment. Six weeks after they had arrived in Milwaukee, Bob and Smithy boarded a jet for the trip back to Detroit.

Smithy's recovery was slow, and the first six months were particularly difficult. Often, he got extremely tired. But slowly, he got his energy back. He was used to being on the go, and more often than not, he mustered the energy to go to the plays Sara directed, to parties and other functions.

Those days, when Sara directed a play at St. Dunston's, they always had the cast over for an "afterglow" party after one of the performances. Smithy would set food out on the buffet that he had arranged with artistic precision. He also spent a lot of time attending meetings at Wayne State and chairing the Arts Council Triangle, a tri-county arts committee. "These meetings were very demanding and even though he seemed fatigued, he would never allow that to hinder him from attending," Sara says. "He was alert while he was on the go, but at home he would read a great deal and watch television."

Smithy had always wanted to go to Taliesin West for Easter because he'd heard they had a great celebration there every Easter. So in April, 1984, he and Sara traveled to Scottsdale, Arizona, where they stayed with their friend Esther Kunin, the wife of Larry Kunin, who had helped so much on their house and who had recently died. After their visit, they drove the short distance to Taliesin. "People from all over the world attended," Sara says. "A few days before Easter, they prepare a bread called Baba bread. People handle the dough and have fun throwing it up in the air, catching it and throwing it on to the next person. I think it was a tradition Mrs. Wright brought from her country. This bread was always served at Easter Sunday brunch. It tasted pretty good, and since everyone had handled that Baba bread, everyone looked forward to eating it.

"When we traveled west, we usually went on to California to visit friends, but that year, Smithy didn't want to go. We did visit our niece, Elaine, and her husband in Tucson, Arizona, but then we went home. Smithy didn't feel well, but he never complained. He went about his activities and oversaw some landscaping. He loved being on his tractor and cutting the grass and taking care of things around the house.

"Every June, we held the Cody High School retiree luncheon. Everyone would bring food, and we always had a great time. But I noticed Smithy wasn't quite as active as usual. No one else was aware of it, but as the day wore on, even though he kept going, he got more and more tired. Then one night in late June, Smithy awakened me and said he thought he had a serious problem, and asked me to walk through the house with him. As we walked, he said that he thought he should check in at the hospital and take tests to see what was causing his drowsiness. So he made arrangements to go into the hospital on July 4th. At the time, Bobby and Anne were traveling in Europe.

Two days before Smithy was scheduled to go into the hospital for tests, an artist named Glenn Michaels came over with a mosaic sculpture made out of mosaic tiles, pieces of metal and wood that Smithy had commissioned. Previously Smithy had purchased an accordion screen from Michaels made of similar, colorful materials that separated the kitchen work area from the dining room. They also had a small piece by Michaels at the west end of the living area. The new piece, a three-dimensional triptych, came in three parts called "The Seven Arts" and would hang above the fireplace.

On that particular day, July 2nd, Michaels brought two of the three parts to the house to put them up. "I remember Smithy sitting at the end of the lounge directing Michaels on where, exactly, the pieces should be placed," Sara says. "Glenn later told me that he had been working so hard on these pieces—he'd been working day and night because he felt such a push to finish them. Now I understand why. Smithy would never have seen them otherwise. Because two days later, on July 4th, Smithy left for the hospital.

Doctors began the tests immediately to determine what was wrong, and Sara promised Bob that she would notify him by phone as soon as Smithy got his test results. "Smithy entered the hospital on July 4th to get his tests," Sara says. "We had hoped he would be released in a few days so he could attend his 50th high school reunion. We were thrilled because our friend Richard Lapin, the friend who'd made my wedding dress, was coming from New York and we all would be together.

"But after the tests, the doctors determined that Smithy had a valve problem, so he was not released. Instead, he was moved into the cardiology wing. Since Bobby had been calling me once or twice a day from Europe, I told him what the doctors said, and he and Anne immediately booked a return flight. The doctors planned to operate on July 30th. So Bobby and I would go to the hospital every day and stay until closing time and even later."

On one of the last days before the operation, Smithy asked Bob to bring him the Frank Lloyd Wright Foundation plans for the new Japanese tea house he had planned to build. When Bob took in the design, Smithy spent an hour or two looking at the tea house, and he said how excited he would be, when he got out of the hospital, to build that tea house on his property.

On the day before the operation, Smithy, Bob and Sara watched the opening ceremony of the 1984 summer Olympics in Los Angeles on television. During that ceremony, the U.S. Olympic athletes paraded around the field holding the American flag, and then they stood at attention while *The Star Spangled Banner* was played. Smithy felt so inspired that, with all these wires coming out of his body and with all the tubes attached to him, he had enough energy to sit up in bed and salute the American flag. He turned to Bob and to Sara and said, 'I'm so proud to be an American.'"

That same day, Smithy requested—and got—a juicy corned beef sandwich that he thoroughly enjoyed. He also had many visitors, and he was filled with enthusiasm and had lively conversations with everyone. Two of his visitors were Marie Guyton, who once had been Sara's principal, and Sophie Plopa, whom Smithy and Sara had met years before when Sophie had sold two dresses to Sara in a fancy dress shop. Smithy had made the selections, but Sara and Sophie had instantly liked one another, and Sara had invited Sophie and her husband to lunch. This turned out to be the beginning of what both couples considered a beautiful friendship. Later on, when Sophie was widowed, she spent even more time with Sara and Smithy, who sometimes included Sophie and Marie on their excursions. At the time, the four were planning a trip to Toronto.

"When I went to see Smithy that Sunday, the day before the surgery, and he was talking about the surgery, I thought, 'Oh no,'" Sophie says. "But he said, 'I'm going to be all right. And don't you worry, because I'm going to have this done, and then we'll travel. Don't worry! We're still going to take that Toronto trip.' And I said, 'Okay, I won't worry; I'll pray.' When I was kissing him good-bye, he says, 'Now don't forget, as soon as I get out of here and get well, we're going to Toronto—Marie, Sara, and you and I.' And I said, 'I'm looking forward to it. Now, don't let me down.' And he held my hand, and he said, 'We're going to Toronto, and the bill is on me.'"

Sophie said, "Oh, that's better yet."

Before Smithy was taken away for surgery, Sara sat in a chair close by, holding his hand, and Bob sat on the bed. Smithy turned to Sara and said, "I will love you through eternity." After a moment of silence, he added, "I'm so happy I married you." And a few moments later: "I respect your Christian Science—stay with it."

Bobby accompanied Smithy into the surgical waiting room. The last thing Bobby remembers is kissing his dad on the forehead and saying, "Dad, you'll be all right. We'll all be waiting for you when it's over. I love you very much, and I thank you for all you've done for me." Bobby then joined his mom in the waiting room along with Anne and some of his cousins.

Following Smithy's surgery, the report was that the valve replacement was successful, but that Smithy had not stopped bleeding. "The doctors pulled me aside to tell me that dad's heart would not stop bleeding," says Bob. "They said it was touch and go. I immediately went back into the waiting room and said, "Mom, we better pray, because Dad needs our help." As we continued to wait, more cousins joined us in the waiting room. One of my cousins started calling the other cousins to let them know things weren't looking too good.

Finally, a nurse named Jeanine Patel, who was a friend of the family's and had taken care of Smithy in Wisconsin, came to talk to me. "She asked me to come downstairs near the operating room," Bob remembers. "I followed her, shaking all the way. When I arrived outside the operating room, the doctor who had performed the surgery came out and told me that they had lost him. There was no way that they could stop the bleeding. They had tried everything, but it just wouldn't stop. His body just couldn't take it, and it gave out.

"I asked to see him, but they didn't want me to. Jeanine said, 'Bobby, remember him like you do when he was alive. Don't go into the room.' I asked her to give me a lock of his hair, and then she went to get my mom.

"I held my mom in my arms, and I told her that Dad was gone. She said, 'He's in God's hands.' We both cried. She said, 'I know he's in his next phase of life. I'll see him again,' she said. 'We'll never leave each other.'

"When we went home, the kids were waiting up," Bob says. "They ran over to me and gave me a big hug. I told them their grandpa had died, and we all cried. Dad was the first person they'd loved who wasn't there anymore."

At the memorial service for Smithy on August 5, 1984, some 300 people gathered on the grounds outside the beautiful Frank Lloyd Wright home Smithy had loved so well. They looked over the serene pastoral site of rolling hills and pond where so many of them had attended parties, piano concerts, outdoor theater and dance performances. It was a beautiful, sunny day. Before the service began, Wesley Peters, president of the Frank Lloyd Wright Foundation, who had become the chief architect for Taliesen after Frank Lloyd Wright's death, walked around the property with Bob and architect Fred Bidigare. Peters admired the sunroom and terrace that had been added in 1968. As they walked, Peters talked about the philosophy of architecture and how much Frank Lloyd Wright had enjoyed Smithy as a client. He also paced out the spot for the recently designed Japanese teahouse Smithy had always wanted. "What else would your dad want me to be doing right now?" Peters asked Bob.

During the service, Peters spoke of how the success of Frank Lloyd Wright's buildings was fostered by personal contact between the owner and the architect—and, in particular, how important Wright's relationship with the Smiths had been in the creation of his "little gem." "Frank Lloyd Wright had much more wealthy clients," said Peters. "He had ones who had much bigger estates or buildings; he had clients who came to him with sites that were superb. But he never had a client who was greater in devotion and love and appreciation than Mr. and Mrs. Melvyn Maxwell Smith, and I think this was reflected throughout both their lives. It was a two-way road because Frank Lloyd Wright appreciated and drew life from all its sources. So when he got more, he gave more, which made a double gain for both architect and owner. Theirs was a relationship Frank Lloyd Wright appreciated all of his life, just as I'm certain it was one that was appreciated by Smithy all of his life."

A string quartet played chamber music by Tchaikovsky and speakers from Wayne State University, the Cranbrook Academy and Taliesen praised Smithy's contributions, humor and insights. And Bob talked of Smithy, "a dreamer who dreamed about leaving this world a more beautiful place than he found it," who had taught for 38 years in the Detroit public school system.

"Dad believed that he was put on earth to help people better understand the beauty of the world in which they lived," Bob said. "And oh, what beauty he brought into people's lives through this house, through his teaching and through his love for the arts and as a patron of the arts. Dad was a man of purpose who always knew his course in life. He was a perfectionist who had no patience for those who lacked the desire to achieve the best from their abilities, and yet he was kind and generous and always willing to help others succeed with their dreams. Dad had a great enthusiasm for life. And he lived life to its fullest; he lived, as Thoreau said in Walden, 'deliberately, deeply . . . sucking all the marrow out of life.'

"It was among the trees, along the streams, that he found his best communion with God," said Bob. "Some of you knew Dad since his high school days at Northern High, where he was a cheerleader. And you know he was always encouraging, always supporting, always a cheerleader stirring the spirit within people for the causes he supported . . ."

Throughout the afternoon, Sara, who greeted everyone with hugs and comforting words, focused on Smithy's words, "I will love you through eternity."

If you would, indeed, behold the spirit of death, open your heart wide unto the body of life, for life and death are one, even as the river and sea are one. In the depth of your hopes and desires lies your secret knowledge of the beyond, and like seeds dreaming beneath the snow, your heart dreams of spring. Trust the dreams, for in them is hidden the gate to eternity.

. . . For what is it to die but to stand naked in the wind and to melt into the sun? And what is it to cease breathing, but to free the breath from its restless ties that it may rise and expand and seek God unencumbered? Only when you drink from the river of silence shall you indeed sing, and when you have reached the mountain top, then shall you begin to climb, and when the earth shall claim your limbs, then shall you truly dance.

From *The Prophet* by Kahlil Gibran,
read at Melvyn Maxwell Smith's memorial service,
August 5, 1984

Chapter 20

ANOTHER CHAPTER
FOR SARA

AFTER SMITHY'S DEATH, Sara didn't falter in her embrace of life. She missed Smithy's physical presence, but she refused to mourn or feel sorry for herself. Smithy was very much alive in her mind, very much with her. "When a ship sails into the horizon and is out of sight, it still exists," she says with a radiant smile. "Isn't that true? Life is eternal. And we just live on, and we progress mentally. I know there's so much to learn. Well, Smithy is still here, too. He's just in the next room."

As always, Sara began her mornings by reading her spiritual material and by writing Bob a note for the day on a sheet of 5x7 white paper—inspirational thoughts to guide him through the challenges he would meet on a daily basis. Sara had been writing him these daily thoughts since he left for college in 1962, and no day went by when she didn't write him one. Bob estimates that he has 10,000 pages of her thoughts and prayers. She also wrote notes to Michael, Anne, Jennifer. She answered correspondence as well, jotting off letters and prayers of encouragement to other friends and people who might need some inspirational thoughts. During the day, she did her work—reading, thinking and taking phone calls from people who sought her counsel. She also continued to go out with her many friends to lunches, plays, concerts, galleries and museums. An entourage of friends picked her up and took her wherever she was going. On Wednesday nights and Sundays, as usual, she went to church services.

Every night, she slept at Bob and Anne's. After dinner, either Bob would go to her house, pick her up and take her back to his house, or if she was out, her friends would drop her off at their home. Bob did not want her spending the night alone. He wanted her where he and his family could spend time with her and make sure that she was secure.

Sara didn't consider herself fragile. If anything, at 77 she was more free and gregarious than ever. She often invited old friends, as well as new people she had just met, to her house for lunch or dinner, where she would offer to stir up something to eat. Her friends, as well as her nephews and nieces, describe these meals with laughter. Without Smithy to help determine the menu, Sara could be as creative and unconventional as she liked. "Sara's idea of cooking is always making wonderful concoctions," says one dear friend with a chuckle. "She opens a variety of cans of Campbell's soup, puts them all together, throws in some mashed potatoes, cheddar cheese and sugar—always sugar—and you get this pot of whatever moved her," says another. Meals or afternoon visits at Sara's were always accompanied by chocolate and Sara's legendary hot fudge sundaes—delicious and very, very sweet.

During these visits, Sara would focus her bright blue eyes on friends and new acquaintances alike and ask with genuine interest, "And how *are* you?" The age of the visitor never altered Sara's interest or attention. Milt and Annie Aptekar say that their daughter Lucy has never forgotten how years before Sara had invited her to take off her shoes and slide around on the floor, and then sat down on the banquette and read stories to her. "No one we know ever did that to any of our children—to have taken the time and to be so thoughtful," says Annie. "Lucy talks about her and thinks about her a great deal. She always thought of Sara as a fairy godmother because she has such a soft, gentle voice." And seven years ago, at a party celebrating Milt and Annie's 50th wedding anniversary, Sara met Lucy's 5-year-old son, Ren. "At our table, Sara was sitting next to Ren," says Annie, "and she talked to him and she read stories to him. No one else at that party—and there were a lot of people there—would have paid attention to Ren to the extent of sitting down and giving him her fullest attention."

Sara's interest, and her ability to listen, is considered by many to be something of an art form, rarely encountered. And her openness is nearly mythic. People call Sara when they are worried, when they are sick, when they're going through divorces, when they're making big decisions, when they want insight or comfort. She spends hours on the phone listening, counseling and sharing her philosophy: *There is no spiritual error. In God's eyes, we are all perfect human beings. We are perfect and complete.* "We reflect eternal life," she says. "We represent infinite mind, the sum of all substance. God is perfect and we are made in his image.

"Every challenge is an opportunity," she counsels. "Isn't that interesting? When we have a challenge, it's an opportunity to know that our dear Father's going to show us how to meet it. So, we have nothing to worry about. We never have to be concerned about anything. All we have to be concerned about is listening, loving, and obeying what we hear. Oh how important loving is."

She advises, "When you meet up with discord, react with love, and before you know it, your enemy will be your best friend. Isn't that wonderful? We don't have any enemies. We only have friends, and we only express love."

Sara lived her beliefs. One time when some houses in the neighborhood were being broken into, Bob had instructed his mother not to answer the door. "Sara and I had been sitting at the table having dinner when the doorbell rings," Sophie Plopa remembers. "I said, 'We're not answering it; Bobby said not to answer.' Then the knock came on the door. I said, 'Well, I'll take a peek through the window.' I tiptoed over to the door and peeked out. I said, 'Sara, it's a young man and he's got jogging shorts on and he seems like a halfway decent kid. So Sara came and she says, 'Why not let him in?' We asked his name and he says, 'I'm Michael Epstein. I live not too far from here, but I jog around here and I admire this house all the time.'

"So Sara says, 'Let's let him in.' So he came in of course, and we made him an iced tea and asked him if he wanted dinner. He became one of our best friends. He used to come over here all the time, and he'd take us to Royal Oak to the new restaurants that opened down there. And he and his friends, about five of them, took Sara and me out on the town several times. Five fellas and two old gals. We went to supper clubs and jazz clubs. They were full of surprises."

On many nights long before his children became teenagers, Bob would find himself waiting up for his mother to come home from her evenings out. One night after midnight, he saw his mother pull up in a red Corvette after having been out for dinner and a discussion with a handsome young man in his 30's, who looked a lot like George Hamilton. They were friends from church, and they'd been oblivious to the time. Clearly, age was no obstacle to their communication. The young man said to Bob, 'You know your mom attracts beautiful women who all want to meet her, so that's another bonus for me."

Another incident during this period was particularly illustrative of Sara's philosophy. It happened one evening when Bob came over after dinner to pick up his mother and take her back to their house for the night. Right after he walked in, the phone rang. "I figured it was probably one of her friends calling for a little spiritual advice late at night," Bob recalls. "I hear Mom pick up the phone, and she says, 'What? What? I don't understand what you're talking about. What?' And this look passes over my mother's eyes, and I realize first, this was not a kind phone call. Then this look of wonderment comes over her face, and Mom says, 'Now you must be feeling very badly to be saying such a thing . . . You seem to be somebody who would like to talk. I would love to talk with you.' It continues on. I finally realize, *this is an obscene phone call.* I said to my mom, 'Just hang up.' She put her finger up in the air to say, 'Wait a minute.' Then she returned to him and finally said to the caller, 'Let's talk about love, let's talk about life.'

"And I'm sitting down, I say, 'Mom just hang up the phone. We all know what you do when you get an obscene phone call. You hang up the phone. You don't talk to him.'"

"But she whispers to me, 'This person needs my love.'

"I said, 'Not the kind of love he's talking about. Mother, this is not a normal person.' You could hear the guy talking in the background. I'm saying, 'Oh, my God!' And she whispers to me, 'This person needs to talk, and I just need to talk with him.'

"Forty-five minutes go by, and she and this person are having quite a conversation. After 15 minutes, she's laughing. By then, they are having a two-way conversation. And the last 15 minutes of it, there is Mom talking to this person spiritually. At the end, I hear this man sobbing on the phone. Literally sobbing. You could hear him crying, saying he's sorry, saying he loves this person on the other end of the phone. He's saying he just can't imagine what he was doing, and he just can't believe that this wonderful person answered his phone call.

"Then, I hear my mother say—as she has done many times, 'Let's get together for lunch on Sunday. Let's have lunch together.' She makes an appointment, gives him a time and location, and I'm almost passing out. She says 'I love you,' and she hangs up the phone.

"I said, 'Mom, what have you done?' She says, 'You know, this is somebody who I really could help. I might have a chance to help him change.' I said, 'God bless you, but I'm going to be there with you.' The man never did show up, but the story really represents the essence of my mother. No matter what problems you have, no matter what burdens you carry, no matter what flaws you possess, my mother stands ready with an open hand and an open heart to help you, to listen to you, to comfort you, and, most important, to love you unconditionally."

After Smithy's death, one of Sara's many friends who stopped in to visit with Sara, often shopped for her, and sometimes drove her to different events was Barbara Kacy, a high school classmate of Bob's who had begun working for him in 1983, shortly after he had purchased his first television station and had opened an office in Birmingham. Barbara and Bob actually had been in school together since the fourth grade. They weren't close friends in either grade school or high school, but they had known each other and had met up again when they worked on their 20th high school reunion. At the time, President Carter was out of the White House, and Bob and Anne had returned to Michigan. Bob had been in the process of figuring out what he wanted to do next, and since both he and Barbara happened to have free time, they became co-chairs of the reunion. They enjoyed working together, and so when Bob heard that Barbara was thinking about going back to work, he offered her a job.

"Bob was the entrepreneur, bringing the deals together and negotiating them, and he said he thought it was unprofessional for him to answer his own phones," Barbara says. "Michelle, my youngest, is Jennifer's age, and I had always been at home for my children. So I'd take Michelle to school, and go to the office, which was ten minutes away. And then I'd leave around three or so. If there was a Halloween program or Valentine's Day or anything like that, Bob was so easy and so good about it. He always said, 'Family comes first,' because in great part, he reflected his mom's philosophy of life. He always said, 'You need to be with your children for special events. It's more important than work.'

"From the beginning, my job description involved Sara and Jennifer and Michael," says Barbara, who in addition to being Bob's administrative assistant soon became an ex-officio member of the Smith family. "If Mike had a tennis lesson and Anne was teaching or whatever, I filled in the gaps where I needed to."

In the late 1980s, when Smith Broadcasting began to grow, Bob, Anne, Jennifer and Michael began to spend summers in Santa Barbara, and Sara often would go with them for a couple of weeks or even a month. But much as she enjoyed her stays, Sara preferred to be at her house, My Haven, on Pon Valley Road. When Sara was in Michigan, however, Bob insisted that she sleep at night in his downtown office apartment, where she had her own room. She spent the days at her house, but slept at the apartment, which meant that Barbara Kacy could check in with her in the mornings.

"She did leg exercises every morning," says Barbara. "She'd be up on her bed pumping her legs, doing the bicycle, and no matter how weak she was, she would never say, I can't do it. She always has been really determined to maintain her strength."

Sara's strength and stamina were extraordinary, particularly given the fact that about a year after Smithy's death, she, too, had almost died. The day in 1985 that it happened, Jeanine Patel, the nurse who had taken care of Smithy, stopped by in the morning. Jeanine had left her job at the hospital when Bob hired her to take care of Sara full time. On this particular morning when Jeanine arrived, she found Sara lying, apparently lifeless, on the bed. Jeanine tried to wake her, but Sara could not be roused. She felt totally cold to the touch, and her eyes were glazed over. Jeanine tried to take her pulse, but could not find one.

"Jeanine called her boss, the heart surgeon who had operated on Smithy, and he came rushing over to the house," Bob recalls. "She called me at work, and the doctor and I got there at the same time. The doctor looked at Mom and said, 'I don't know if she can make it another hour.' He said, 'If it were up to me, I would immediately put her on life support to get her heart rate back to normal. I think I can get it back to where it's working again, but her heart is so weak that she desperately needs a pacemaker. I don't think she can make it without one.

"He said, 'I'd like to have the permission to get her to the hospital, because she can't make any decisions now. At least it would give her a chance.' I asked him what her prospects were, and he said, 'My guess is—I can't tell you for sure—but without intervention, she probably won't make it for very long. She's not pumping much blood. She cannot stay like this—she's not getting enough oxygen to her brain. I can't even get a pulse out of her. I can hardly hear her heartbeat.'

"Tears now were pouring out of my eyes. I held her and I said, 'Okay, Mom, here's the issue. You gotta listen to me. This is Bobby talking.' I said, 'The doctor is here and says that there is a chance he can save you if he can get you to the hospital. Can you hear me?' She did not move. 'Can I have him take you to the hospital?' And out of nowhere, I basically get a slight shaking of the head no. I said, 'Doctor, she hears me.' He said, 'I can't believe that, but yes, I saw it.' I said, 'Okay, Mom, if you're saying no, I'm going to give this another little while, and then after that I can't deal with it any more. I've got to try and save you. I'm going to get your practitioner on the phone. I'm going to put this phone next to your ear, and all I want you to do is listen. Whatever you do, please listen. I cannot let you die.'

"So I called up the practitioner and told him what was going on. He said, 'Just put the phone by her ear.' So I cradle my mom, and he's talking and talking, and he's praying, and Mom's listening. One of the things he kept saying was, "There is no imperfection in God. We have within ourselves strength and our own control. Everything is perfect. Your heart is perfect. Your body is perfect.'

"And the doctor is holding her wrist and he says, 'I'm getting a little pulse. Whatever this guy is doing, let him keep doing it.' Jeanine says,

'There's movement now.' So, we're all three there. And the practitioner kept talking and talking, and Mom slowly, slowly kept responding. I forgot what time it was, but the doctor canceled all his appointments, and Jeanine was there and we all just sat there watching Mom. Over a two-hour period, my mom developed a temperature again, developed normal blood pressure, and her eyes went from glassy and glazed over to focused again. And within a couple hours, she was up walking around and was normal again.

"The doctor said, 'I have never ever in my life seen anything like this. I've never gone through an experience like this. She was basically gone.' I said, 'Doctor, what would you suggest?' He said, 'Let me tell you what I suggest. I'd say you have a miracle here. I'd also say I would get her in to the hospital as soon as possible and get her a pacemaker. I think with a pacemaker she would have a better chance to last longer. That's my medical opinion. After what I've just seen, I don't know what to tell you. She could drop over in five minutes and die, and you should not be shocked. She could live another six months to a year, and you shouldn't be shocked. And she could live longer than that. But she has the weakest of hearts. It basically is not able to carry her any more. She needs help, but that does not account for what faith does.'

"The doctor said, 'There's no medical way to explain what I have just seen,'" Bob recounts. "'You hear about it in class, you read about it,' he said, 'but now I've seen it. So I cannot tell you what to do. But she is now up, and she's walking around, she's going to the bathroom. I just can't believe it. You don't need me here any more. There's nothing that my training can do here.' Before he left, he told Bob, 'I can't tell you if she has one more day or one more month or one more year to live. Any time you now have with her is a special gift.'"

Bob shakes his head remembering this event. "Every day since then, *every* day," he says, "I've figured God has just given me that much of a blessing. Every single day has been this miracle that she was able to overcome death. I've asked her, 'Did you see anything? Did you feel anything?' And she says, 'I just was at peace. I was just at peace. I wasn't afraid.' I said, 'Did you know what was happening?' She says she didn't quite know what was happening. But she had been so trained in prayer that her mind latched onto the prayers and to the idea that she was in perfect condition, her heart was perfect, and it got her to the point where she consciously or subconsciously could solve the problem. And I'm telling you, I saw it myself, but to this day I still do not believe what I witnessed."

"By filling your thoughts with good," says Sara,
"you will find there is no room for evil."

Chapter 21

THE POPCORN PLAYERS

Sara not only recovered, but she moved forward with vigor. In thinking about her days, she had realized that what she was missing was a deeper involvement with children and with the theater. Most of all, she missed her work as Assistant Director of the Cranbrook Summer Theater, where she had taught drama and directed musical shows for children for sixteen summers. She had given up Cranbrook in 1965 when Smithy had told her that if she went back to Cranbrook that summer, he would start traveling alone. "Because I worked all during the winter and then was occupied all summer, it was a little bit too much for Smithy," Sara says. "But I had resigned very sorrowfully, really." Afterwards, some of the actors she had worked with at the summer theater urged her to join St. Dunston's Theater Guild at the Cranbrook Institute, where she was readily accepted, and where she had stayed active, working on committees, acting, and directing plays.

Often, she ran into former students who told her how much they had loved working with her, how it had changed them—and this made her nostalgic. Their parents, as well as other actors and theatre people also commented regularly about Sara's brilliance as an actor and director. Sara knew there was a reason people were talking to her about her talent and verve, and about how good she was at teaching children to have fun in school *and* in life. They were reminding her of her natural gift for this work—and, unknowingly, encouraging her to continue using this gift.

In 1985, Sara approached Jan Bird, the program director at Birmingham's Community House, with the idea of a Saturday morning Youth Theater. She told Jan that she had been directing fewer plays at

St. Dunston's Theater Guild and was eager to work with young people again. What Sara didn't know was that just recently, the staff of Community House had been trying to figure out how to establish a year-round performing arts program for young people in the community.

"Sara was like our Mary Poppins who came out of the blue, out of the sky with her umbrella, just when we needed her," says Gale Caldwell, who became director of Community House in 1983. "We had this dream of expanding our summer performing arts camp into the school year, but we didn't have the resources to go out on our own and find someone to lead us. Who would have guessed that this special and talented 80-year-old woman would come into our lives and do just what we needed to have done at that time? It must have been fate because this was our dream and our vision.

"As a grassroots organization, we never could have afforded someone of Sara's capability, who impacted the community so much. Everyone knew of Sara, what she had done with theater and with children. And here she was, with her fine reputation in our community, looking around for a place to use her talents. Fortunately, she chose us. We were so excited to have someone of this stature who was willing to embark on this venture with us."

With such an enthusiastic response from the Community House, Sara quickly set up Saturday morning youth theater classes and drew in a team of three young acting instructors from Wayne State to work with her. In this way she launched "The Popcorn Players" and began teaching hundreds of children many of the dramatic techniques she herself had learned during her Saturday morning classes in the 1930s. Sara's daughter-in-law Anne, who by then had taught drama for 18 years in schools, first in Maryland and then in Michigan, says Sara's staging and directing were particularly brilliant. "Sara always said there has to be constant motion on the stage, which I agree with," says Anne. "She also taught me a method of blocking movement across the stage, and how to work with big groups. Her method is foolproof—however large a group —three kids or 100 kids. You say, 'All right, this is position number one,' and you set the kids in that position. You say, 'This is position two,' and so on up to 35 positions. The kids just memorize the positions with the numbers and where it comes in the lines, which is so great.

"Now some people say this is too contrived, and you should let the actor elicit the emotion, but this gives the children structure. They can move within that structure. If you look at Sara's blocking sheet, you'll see six different movements. So whenever she sees anything on the stage, she's always looking for the movements, and I am, too. I learned that from her."

As Michael and Jennifer grew older, they, too, had gotten involved with their grandma's theater world. Michael remembers how happy his grandma was when her young actors put on a show. "I remember sitting next to her while she was directing one of the plays," Michael recalled. "I'd look over at her and she was just beaming. She shined, even more than normal. And after the show, she was so happy. I think that plays were her calling—definitely her passion and her love. When she got the opportunity to be part of St. Dunston's and Popcorn Players, she was so happy. And it was great for me to see her that way.

"Once I actually acted in one of her plays for the Popcorn Players. And she was a tough director. She took it seriously, but at the same time, she was very encouraging. I also remember as a kid having just hundreds of people come up to me and say, 'Your grandma's the best!' At the time, it didn't really strike me, but now, you can see what kind of great woman you're dealing with."

As a child, Jennifer regularly performed in her school plays and also was in a group called the Peanut Butter Players, a professional children's theater group that did some 72 performances a year. She remembers her grandmother helping her practice her parts, helping with diction, giving advice on how to breathe, and how to emphasize and project her words. "She taught me how magical a stage could become," says Jennifer. "I remember many nights she would stay up late, helping me memorize lines for plays I was in. She also always helped me with my blocking."

Although Jennifer chose to major in telecommunications rather than drama when she went to college at Pepperdine University, she still loves the whole business. "I got the love of the theater from my grandmother and from my mother," she says. "Through them, my love for the theater blossomed. That was a special gift that they passed on to me."

Other students who worked with Sara find that they, too, still use what they learned from her. "Sara just brings a smile to everyone whose life she has touched," says Gale Caldwell. "She was always here, every Saturday morning, to work with the children. She expected them to practice their skills, not only on the stage, but in everyday life. She was always here to look them in the eye and shake their hands, and she wanted that presence to be something they carried away from class. She took kids who maybe didn't have a lot of confidence and allowed them to really shine and flourish. She gave them the courage to stand up in front of an audience. Her respect for each child gives them the opportunity to grow, to develop a self-respect, a self-image and self-awareness. Those things that you learn young in life really help you in whatever you do.

"Sara also has an uncanny ability to spot talent, and she's a very generous loving person as well. If there was anything she could do to further a young person's career, she was willing to do that in a very loving, no-strings-attached way."

So began a long-lasting love affair between Sara and the Community House in Birmingham, Michigan. And what Sara started has grown and still is being passed on to young people there. After Sara started the Popcorn Players Theatre School on Saturday mornings, her students worked toward a scheduled performance, a small play at the end of each session that involved costumes and staging. Sara's dream was to have bigger productions at the Community House, and to put on full-scale musicals. But it took a while to build the program, and in the meantime, other life events intervened.

Something quite unexpected was a move to the West Coast. In 1991, business and other family needs necessitated a full-time move to California for Bob, Anne, Jennifer and Michael, and it became clear that Sara eventually would have to move west with the rest of the family. For a while, she spent six months in Michigan working with the Popcorn Players and six months with the family in California, where she also produced children's plays at the Howard School in Montecito.

But in November, 1994, she moved permanently to Santa Barbara.

Nevertheless, Sara didn't by any means abandon her dream of having full-scale productions at Birmingham's Community House. Beginning in the fall of 1995, the year after Sara moved west, the drama program expanded to include not only the Popcorn Players Theatre School, but a new venture named the Sara Smith Productions, a program dedicated to major productions starring children. Sara Smith Productions mounted two full-length productions during its first year. The very first play was *Robin Hood*, quickly followed by *Aladdin*. Then came *Cinderella*, *Willie Wonka*, *The Wizard of Oz*, *Peter Pan*, and *Annie*.

"This program started very small," says Peggy Kerr, youth director at the Community House, who now oversees the staff and children involved in the bi-annual productions. "At our first show, we had a small, intimate gathering—maybe 25 kids and our audience consisted of maybe 50 to 75. And now our audiences number two to three hundred, generally sold-out performances."

And even though Sara isn't physically present, her presence is felt—by Peggy and the musical director, costume mistress, acoustic director, and choreographer, as well as the children—to whom Sara's teaching is, quite literally, being passed on. One of her students from the late 80s, for instance, Rossano Rea, recently was an assistant director for the Community House's production of *The Wizard of Oz*. "Rossano's beyond his years," says Peggy. "He started here as a young child and gained a lot of confidence working with Sara. He was in the Popcorn Players, and then he was in the first plays that were here. Since then, he has been assistant director. He has a lot of feelings for Sara, and talks about her a lot.

"Last spring somebody who worked here was teaching the kids how to breathe, and he and Rossano had a misunderstanding. Rossano came up to me, and he was almost in tears. He said, 'Peggy, that's not how I learned it. Sara taught me to do it *this* way. And I want the kids to know it because that's how I did it, and that's how Sara did it, and that's how they should do it.' He's very passionate about what he learned from her."

Peggy Kerr sends programs, T-shirts, and pictures from the performances to Sara. "One day last spring in March, we called up Sara," says Peggy. "I said, 'Sara, this is Peggy Kerr. I've been writing you, and I wanted to talk to you over the phone.' She knew right away who I was. She said, 'Oh, I love everybody there. Tell them I send my love.' I said, 'Sara. I really want you to talk to some of the kids who are in the play.' And so, I put Katy Marshall on the phone, and she said, 'I'm Katy, and I'm working in the play.' They had a conversation, and then afterwards, they started writing, and they became pen pals. Katy wants Sara to know how much she's gained from this experience.

"It is so rewarding to see thirty kids come in, and a lot of them don't know each other, and when they leave, they've developed friendships," says Peggy. "And that's the most important thing. They've developed friendships and self-esteem. And the parents are saying, 'I can't believe this. The best thing has happened to my child.' And they're really sincere about it. They know how much work went into it.

"Also, the parents see their child coming home every day—and they see that their child can't wait to go to rehearsal the next day. It's very rewarding to see the whole process come together. And then when the production is over, it's a let-down. You want to keep it going. But then you start fresh again with a new play, so it just keeps going."

"Sara's legacy is carried on vicariously through people, from children she's taught to members of the staff," says Gale Caldwell. "It's carried on from Jan Bird to Michelle to Peggy, our youth director who's implementing Sara's philosophy, and it hasn't gotten lost. Her message is so strong that it's carried on to generations of people who don't know her, and that's hard to do."

In 1997, Bob and Anne Smith gave a gift to the Community House that established The Sara Evelyn Smith Stage. They did this in honor of Sara's 90th birthday—to insure that long into the future, Sara's presence will remain on stage.

"We never have to be concerned about anything," says Sara. "All we have to do is to listen—to listen and love. Oh, how important loving is. Never react to error of any kind, because if you do, immediately there is discord. And there doesn't have to be discord. When you meet up with discord, react with love, and before you know it, your enemy will be your best friend. Isn't that wonderful? We don't have any enemies. We only have friends and we only express love."

Chapter 22

SANTA BARBARA SUNSETS

AT CATE HIGH SCHOOL IN SANTA BARBARA, 16-year-old Michael
Smith sat listening to Holocaust survivor Judith Meisel tell her story.
Ms. Meisel's father died in 1938, shortly after the Russians had occupied Lithuania, and Judith moved with her mother, sister and brother
to the city. Not long after that, the Jews in her town were marched out
by the Nazis and forced to dig their own graves before they were shot.

Altogether, Judith Meisel lost 147 members of her family—43 of
them children—during the Holocaust. She herself was 12 years old
when she and her mother, sister and brother were taken to a Nazi concentration camp. When she was 15, she and her mother were ushered to
the gas chambers, where their heads were shaved. During a screaming
match with the guards, however, Judith's mother managed to push
Judith out of the room before the door was closed. Later, during a death
march to another camp, Judith escaped to Denmark. When she arrived
in Denmark on May 5, 1945, she was 16 years old and weighed 47
pounds. "The Danes immediately put me into a hospital for a year and
a half and nursed me back to health," Ms. Meisel told the students.
"Luckily, my brother survived Dachau—and my sister also survived. We
are part of the six percent of survivors from that ghetto. Six percent."

When Judith Meisel finished talking about her experiences, she
said, "Please respect each other's differences. All of you are able to make
a difference in another person's life. Get an education—because this is
your world, this is your future. It just takes one person caring enough to
make the world a better place."

When Ms. Meisel finished speaking, Michael went up to her and
thanked her for telling her amazing story. "There is someone in my life

I would love for you to meet, if possible," he said. "She's my grandma."

"Your grandmother? Oh, so many people today don't have very much connection with their grandparents."

"My grandma lives with us," Michael said. "She's unbelievably wonderful, and I know you'd like each other."

Soon after that, Anne arranged a tea for Judy Meisel and Sara, who instantly liked each other. "These are two amazing women," Michael said. "I was sitting in the room with them, and there was just an air of grace between the two—and you just felt their power. Judy's just amazing—and my grandmother is unbelievable. So it was really great seeing two women at their best. Two people who are incredible. So I was very happy to bring them together and not surprised at all that they hit it off." Judy and Sara became close friends, and later, when Judy was diagnosed with cancer, she visited Sara every week. Sara would pray with her, and the two would talk about life. "I inspire others," Judy Meisel said. "But Sara is the one who inspires me."

In many ways, it had been Michael who had initiated the family's permanent move to Santa Barbara—a place that the entire family loved. The transition had begun slowly, with summer and winter visits and then holidays in Santa Barbara.

Bob first fell in love with the place in the late 1970s when he was working for the Community Services Administration. He and Joe Kennedy, Bobby Kennedy's oldest son and a former congressman, were driving from San Francisco to Los Angeles on a special project. "Joe said that I should stop in Santa Barbara, which he said was one of the most beautiful cities in the world, to see the Community Action Agency there," Bob recalls. "We arrived just as dusk was falling over the Santa Barbara harbor. Joe and I got out and walked the beautiful sandy beach, and while we were walking, he turned to me and said, 'I knew you would love this place. Some day you'll be back here.'"

More and more as an adult, Bob found himself drawn to Santa Barbara. And more and more, the family enjoyed the California sunshine. Michael, who became a nationally ranked junior tennis player, especially enjoyed it because of its year-round tennis opportunities.

When it came time for his Bar Mitzvah, he wanted it held in Los Angeles. Michael always talked about how much he liked everything in Santa Barbara. At the end of every summer and every holiday, the family would pack up all their belongings and return home. Then one early September day, just when they were ready to fly back to Detroit and everyone had carried their bags down to the door, Michael looked up and said, "I don't understand why we're going back to Michigan."

His question made Bob and Anne realize that, in truth, the family was more emotionally rooted in Santa Barbara than in Birmingham. Jennifer, like Michael, very much wanted the California life. And Michael's acceptance into the eighth grade at Crane Middle School, an excellent private school in Santa Barbara, tipped the scales.

But it also created a dilemma. Anne could stay on the west coast with Michael for the school year, but what would that do to the family? Jennifer was going into her junior year in high school in Michigan. So Bob and Anne gave her a choice. She could stay in Michigan until she graduated from high school or move west. Jennifer hated to leave her friends, but eagerly opted for Santa Barbara. "That left Sara in Michigan and Anne in Santa Barbara with the two kids, and Bob, who is totally devoted to all, right in the middle," Barbara Kacy remembers. "So that was going to be heartbreaking for Bob.'

In retrospect, the shift to the west coast seemed almost inevitable. Since the time Bob had begun his broadcasting career, one of his goals had been to someday own a television station in Santa Barbara. The local station, KEYT, an ABC affiliate, had come up for sale in 1984, but unfortunately, Bob and his group lost the bid to Roy Disney, who was Walt Disney's nephew. There was only one commercial television station licensed to Santa Barbara, so there were no other television options there. If Bob wanted a station in Santa Barbara, he had to have the one owned by Roy Disney. So, for the next three years, Bob called the Roy Disney organization every month to ask whether they would consider selling the station to him. Finally the Disney group, headed by Stanley Gold, told Bob that if he wanted the station, they would sell it to him for the price they named—not a penny less, and he had a week to let them know if they had a deal. Within that week, Bob put together a financial package that would allow him to buy KEYT from the Disney group. He completed its purchase in August of 1987, the same month he and Anne also bought a home in Santa Barbara.

With Anne, Jennifer and Michael at home in Santa Barbara and his mother in Bloomfield Hills working with the Popcorn Players at Community House, Bob flew back and forth between Michigan and California for two years. But in the fall of 1994, Sara was suffering from a deep abscess on her leg which had spread from her ankle to her knee and wouldn't heal. Because of pain from the abscess, Sara was using a walker to help her get around. Bob took her to Santa Barbara, and asked her to see a doctor friend of his for an evaluation, and she agreed. After examining her, the doctor said that the reason the lesion wasn't healing was because she had no circulation in that area of her foot and leg. He warned that gangrene could set in soon, and if it did, she might need to have her leg amputated in order to save her life. Sara said, "Just wait. Are you telling me that if I can get my blood to circulate to my foot, then I would be able to heal the sore?" The doctor said yes, but as it was, the blood wasn't circulating there. Sara said, "Give me three or four days, and I'll come back."

Bob reports that Sara went home and prayed. "Four days later, when she went back," he says, "to the doctor's shock and amazement, the echocardiogram on her leg showed that there was a wonderful blood flow to her foot. The doctor wrapped her leg, and within a couple of months, the abscess was totally healed."

Both Ann and Bob felt that because of Sara's reduced mobility, the time was right for her to stay on, and they told her that they thought her stay should be permanent. Their house was a large one, and they felt there was plenty of room for her to live with them. "It's not easy to bring a mother into a house, and it takes a lot of understanding," Bob acknowledges. "But everybody pitches in. Everybody makes it work. As Mom has blessed all of us, Anne has blessed the relationship between Mom and myself. There are few people who would have been able to allow me to live this dream of sharing my love with my mother, and for that Anne has all my admiration, love and heartfelt thanks."

Michael and Jennifer were particularly thrilled about having their grandmother with them on a full-time basis. "Every morning since I can remember, my grandma has put out a note for me," Michael says. "It might be a prayer, advice, good thoughts, or a simple 'I love you.' Whenever I face the smallest of problems or serious life decisions, my grandmother's there with words of wisdom to help get me through my challenges. She helped me put my life into perspective. I aspire some-day to have some level of the understanding of life that she has. My grandmother is fearless. She's the brightest light I have ever seen—so bright that it will shine in each of us forever. Her message is eternal. It is: *love everyone, hurt no one.* It's so simple, yet so profound. We are lucky because we can all share her vision that 'we are all perfect. We are all beautiful. We all express love.'"

Sara quickly adjusted to her full-time schedule in Santa Barbara —and before long, it seemed she had always been there. Her friendships flourished, and as she became less mobile and more frail, she began to hold court from two of her favorite spots in Bob and Anne's beautiful house—the kitchen and the dining room. To this day, people like Judith Meisel; Judy Weisbart; Mirelle Noone and her daughter Natalie; Susan Bridges and her daughter Haley, and many others make pilgrimages to see Sara. Her friends are a disparate crowd that includes children from the theater, Joseph P. Kennedy II, who exchanges prayers and words of encouragement with her, and author Marianne Williamson, who calls Sara for inspiration.

From her own room, Sara walks into the kitchen nook and table, where she can talk on the phone, write notes to friends and welcome visitors—again, visitors and friends of all ages. "Sara supports her friends wholeheartedly," says Anne. Stories abound about her availabil-ity for prayer and advice. For instance, when a friend of Anne's, Harriet Johnston, wife of Beach Boy member Bruce Johnston, called Sara from England to tell her that a boy on her son's rowing team had hurt his shoulder and the whole crewing team would be disqualified if the boy couldn't row, Sara talked to the young man himself in London. She talked him out of the sensation he was feeling in his shoulder—telling him he was perfect, and that he expressed perfect strength and ability. Sure enough, he was able to row and the team won the championship.

And, despite her religious beliefs, Sara has developed some surprising friendships with two local doctors. Bob first called these physicians, Dr. Tim Spiegel and Dr. Harris Gelberg, when he was concerned about Sara's health. He knew that it was rare for doctors to make house calls, but in this case, Bob knew his mother would never visit them in their offices. Understanding her beliefs, they kindly agreed to periodically visit Sara, and during these visits, they both grew to enjoy her philosophy and outlook on life. "My mom always looks forward to their lunchtime visits," says Bob. "One time when I was thanking Dr. Spiegel for dropping everything to see my mom, he turned to me and said, 'Believe me, she does more for me than I could ever do for her.'"

Sara also maintains a special relationship with Meryl and Monte Brown. She first met them through church, and they are friends who help Sara on many levels. They often share spiritual conversations, and Monte is the person Sara calls when she needs support with a problem. She also enjoys a very close relationship with Virginia Harris, the chairman of the board of the First Church of Christian Science. Sara has known Virginia for decades because they attended the same church in Bloomfield Hills, Michigan. Virginia has visited Sara in Santa Barbara, and the two keep in touch by phone. "Mom and Virginia provide inspiration to each other," says Bob. "They love sharing their philosophies, convictions and adventures."

Michael and Jennifer watch their grandmother's activities with pleasure. "My grandma loves being able to make people happy in any way," says Michael. "One of the ways, even today, that she tries to make people happy is through food. She loves to do that. When any of my friends come over, she's such a typical grandma. She says, 'Can I give you some cookies? Do you want any candy?' We used to make fudge together in the kitchen. All my friends still ask whether my grandma is making fudge.

"This past summer, I had a pretty big party here," Michael says. "And we're down by the pool. It's right around Fiesta time, and everyone's hanging out. A group of friends and I went down to Fiesta, and we're walking around having a good time. But a group of girls wandered up and saw Grandma sitting in the kitchen, and they just started talking to her. So, when I got back, everyone at the party was saying, 'You have the most amazing grandma in the whole world.'

"These were people that I really hadn't talked to, some I hadn't even met, and they were asking, 'What is your family about?' They were just so interested. They were *so* not used to someone like Grandma. She truly wanted to know about them. She was interested in who they were and what they were about. The kids aren't used to getting this from adults—they're not used to getting this with grandparents. Some of their grandparents just say, 'Good seeing you, take care.'

"But she's very real, and people were moved by her to the point where I was sometimes getting calls from random girls saying, 'How's your grandma?' And I'm thinking, 'Wow, what about me?' She's a tough act to follow. At first, visitors come to the house to see us, but then they'll just keep coming back to see her.

"She will bring the most random people together—people who would never typically sit at the same table and have a discussion. And it goes perfectly. It is smooth. And then these people may never see each other again, but, for that time, they're truly on the same level. Everyone's equal with her. There is an absolute connection. Little kids will sit down with adults, and have full conversations, and it'll totally work.

"We're very lucky. Because we've grown up with her, it lives on in all of us. Maybe not in the same magnitude, but the spirit and the idea. I love getting together random people, people who would never be together otherwise, and make it work and have fun."

Jennifer also feels her grandmother's guiding hand on the shape of her life. "When I went to Florence, Italy, for a semester, I didn't think I would see her when I came back," Jennifer says. "She was really sick when I left, and my dad said, 'Make sure you say goodbye.' There's a bunch of times I've had to say goodbye to her, but God keeps giving her back to me. She wrote me this book of all these different sayings that I will keep for always. In it, because she knew I was going to be traveling so much, she wrote, 'God goes before you to prepare the way.' And also, 'God is the pilot of life, of the plane, of everything.'

"So, every time I travel, I say like it's my mantra, 'God is the pilot; he's going before me to prepare the way.' So it is like Grandma is with me every time I fly. And I've told that saying to people who have fears of flying and they're so helped by it. They say, 'Let me write that down.' So it's just little things. Her philosophy, her ideas, have stuck with me and really made me who I am. I think that if I had lost her back when I was ten years old, I would be different, but thanks to her, I'm a very spiritual person."

Anne, who has been president of the Lobero Theatre in Santa Barbara, which is the longest continually running theater in California, says that she, too, has been forever changed by Sara. For one thing, with Sara living in her house, Anne often drives home and sees the cars of friends who have come over—not to see her, but to see Sara. "I never know who is going to be at the house visiting Sara," says Anne. "I try to have luncheons for her with people who should meet her or that she would enjoy because she can't get out anymore. People meet her, and she's so wonderful that they start coming over, and then they keep coming.

"I used to have a mother-daughter tea on Valentine's day, and one year my mother came too, so Sara needed another person to be her 'daughter' at the tea, and I told that to my friend Sondra Tyler and she told it to her friends Jano Stack and Chrissy Waterman, and all three came as Sara's daughters. Ever since then, the 'daughters' take her to lunch or stop by to see her. She has friends of all ages. There's a little two-year-old, for instance, who often asks to go visit Sara, because he knows she always will give him a cookie and a hug. Sara is the lady everybody wants to visit because she has such an incredible capacity for friendships. Everybody remembers Sara, and everybody talks about her."

Anne says that many of Sara's friends remind one another of "Sara-isms," a euphemism for ways to take a positive approach to life. At one point, for instance, when two of Sara's Santa Barbara "daughters," Jano Stack and her sister Chrissy Waterman, were driving across country, each in a van with their kids in it, they got stuck in traffic. One yelled to the other, "Can you believe this blinking *#*!+# traffic?" And the other sister yelled back, "Now that's not a very Sara-like thing to say!"

Anne also got a kick out of the range of Sara's friendships during the 1998 NBA basketball championships. Herb Simon, the owner of the Indiana Pacers, often stopped by to see Sara, and he asked her to say prayers for him and his team through the first two rounds of the playoffs. In the third round against the Chicago Bulls, with the series tied 3 to 3, Sara was watching the seventh game, riveted and absolutely gleeful as the players raced down the court, jumped, slammed into one another. She cheered as the Pacers made a basket. "This is so thrilling," she said. "We're going to win! We're absolutely going to win!" She punched her fists into the air, absolutely radiant. Indiana was in the lead until the final two minutes, when Michael Jordan and his teammates pulled off a stunning victory for the Bulls. Sara was disappointed, but still energized after the game, when Herb Simon called. "Sara," he said with a chuckle, "I want to thank you for all your prayers. But next year, you have to pray a little harder."

"She's how I would like to be as I grow older," says Anne. She's so invested and involved. She affects so many lives. She reaches out. She's the first one we tell when there's a problem, whether it's physical, family, business—anything. If I say to her that I have a stomach ache, she says, 'God's child cannot feel tension. God's child can only feel relaxation and effortlessness. There's no pressure in God's world.' She's able to key into whatever the sensation or physical difficulty is and reverse it. She's saying that we don't need to listen to the carnal mind; that the spiritual body is our real body.

"I remember how, when Smithy was negative about something or was overly demanding, she would say, 'That's not the real you speaking. The real you wouldn't use words like that.' She would work on her own reaction to the person rather than trying to change the person. It's very powerful. And if someone complains to her that they didn't get invited to something, Sara would tell them not to be hurt. She would say, 'There's something else you're supposed to be doing. You're always in the right place.'

"If I have a cold and I say, 'I can't kiss you,' she says to me, 'Only love is contagious. I can only catch love. I can't catch colds.' She takes whatever the common parlance is and changes it to what's spiritual. I call her our resident angel."

In addition to her effect on family and friends in California, Sara's legacy in Michigan continues. In 1997, Sara helped Bob and Anne create the Melvyn Maxwell and Sara Smith Foundation, which assures that their Frank Lloyd Wright home will be open to the public for decades to come, not only as a tribute to the vision, love and dedication they put into building it, but also as an educational and cultural center serving the interests of art and architecture. Frank Lloyd Wright's "little gem"—or My Haven, as Sara and Smithy called it—was declared an historic site in 1998 and listed in the National Register of Historic Places.

Every year, more visitors come through the extraordinary little home. They walk around the grounds and admire the juniper, willow, birch and oak trees, the pond, the sculpture. And when they go inside, they're even more impressed.

Recently, Sara had a good laugh when architect and professor Fred Bidigare told her about a school teacher from Alaska who was visiting the house. The schoolteacher walked around with a look of awe on her face, and then she said, "Two *schoolteachers* did this? I know what I'm going to do! I'm going to go back and demand an increase in my contract! I got the photographs. I got the proof it can be done!"

"Love never dies," says Sara as she talks about Smithy.
"Nothing ever dies."

Chapter 23

FACING THE FUTURE, 1998

Sᴀʀᴀ ɪs sɪᴛᴛɪɴɢ ɪɴ ᴛʜᴇ ʏᴇʟʟᴏᴡ-ᴛɪʟᴇᴅ ᴋɪᴛᴄʜᴇɴ of Bob and Anne's home on Constance Avenue in Santa Barbara. It's 11 a.m., and she looks fresh, almost sparkling, her skin smooth as velvet from her morning shower given to her by her loving aide, Jerma Menders. There's a bright glow around her gleaming white hair, which is as fine and soft as the down on baby geese, still wispy from its washing. Her eyes, bright and alert, sparkling with laughter, sit in a face almost elfin, and her voice sometimes is no more than a whisper. But when she smiles, an enormous brightness fills the room.

Her tiny frame, curled forward from the hips, is clothed in a black and white dress, topped by a white scarf, a pearl necklace, gold chain with a gold heart locket, and gold bracelets. She pulls out her *Daily Reader*, studies the Bible verses, closes her eyes, thinks and prays. Then she pulls out her 5x7 pad of white paper and writes a page of thoughts for Bobby, one of many pages that she will write before this day is over.

Later, in early evening as the sun is going down behind the hills of Santa Barbara, Sara pushes her Mercedes of a walker from the kitchen, where she's been sitting, into the ornate dining room. The walker's stainless steel basket is full of her notes and books, and its thick wheels support her when she stands and moves, gripping the handles and leaning down as she pushes forward. She moves with purpose and intensity, almost as if she were pushing a wheelbarrow to the garden for planting.

Sara used to be only five feet tall, and that was when she was much younger. Now she is bending forward with effort and concentration, making her seem no more, perhaps, than four foot-eight. She moves her walker up to the table, the last to arrive for dinner. Bobby and Anne both rise to help her get seated and comfortable, with pillows at her back, chair scooted close enough to the table.

"We always start our meal with a prayer Mother likes," Bob says, taking Sara's hand. Anne takes Sara's other hand and reaches for Michael's hand. Michael links hands with Jennifer's fiancé, Nicholas; Nicholas takes Jennifer's hand and Jennifer holds her dad's hand. They all bow their heads, linked together as they say out loud:

> *Thank you for the world so sweet.*
> *Thank you for the food we eat.*
> *Thank you for the birds that sing.*
> *Thank you, God, for everything.*

During dinner, Sara stops several times to get her breath, to slow the tension in her chest, to relax her system. "You know I do Bible lessons," she says, "and in this one lesson I read last week, it says, 'We come into the world with nothing and we go out with nothing.' Isn't that so true? Well, I have a joke about that. Would you like to hear it?"

"Yes, yes!" everyone says. "Tell it!"

"All right. There was this man who was extremely wealthy, and he knew he was going to die, and so he called his three best friends in and said, 'I'm going to divide my money and give one-third to each of you. When I die, I want you each to put that money into the casket with me.'

"Well, after he was buried, his three friends got together, and one of them said, 'I was so desperate at the time that I only put half of the money in the casket.' The second friend said, 'It was the same for me. I also only put in half!' The third friend said, 'I put *everything* in. I wrote him out a check for the whole amount!'

"Isn't that funny?" she says. "Think about it! What is money, anyway? When we get a sense of perspective, we know that the joy of living is in giving.'"

At the end of a delicious dinner of pasta, seafood and salad, Sara rises from the table with effort and pushes her walker back toward the kitchen. The trip, even though it's a short one, tires her. She has to stop several times to get her breath, and when she sits, she has to position herself next to the chair and lower herself very very slowly. It's difficult and requires such great exertion that when she sits, she seems to collapse in on herself for a few moments as she recovers her stamina.

Not being able to move quickly, not being able to actively go wherever she wants to go on her own steam, is upsetting to Sara. It's what she calls "a challenge." "I'm a person who used to run everywhere," she says. "And now I'm sitting, I'm not running. I came out here on November 7th, 1994, and I was walking then.

"This lack of activity is a challenge for me. It's a trial. I remember, however, words from one of my favorite hymns: 'Gratitude is riches. Complaint is poverty. My trials bloom in blessing; they test my constancy.' So I am now being tested.

"But," she says, her eyes twinkling in pleasure as a huge and radiant smile breaks out on her face, "I *will* run again. I will! You'll see!"

"God's good never runs out."

— Sara Stein Smith
Santa Barbara, 2000

ACKNOWLEDGEMENTS

THE LAUGHTER, good cheer and serendipity that characterize Sara Smith's life have been contagious during the past two years. I thank Sara for the fun she brought to our many hours of interviews, and for the use of her own memoirs, which were so helpful to me as I wrote this book. I have never met anyone more consistently joyful and expansive than Sara. Her positive temperament is reflected in her remarkable family, particularly in her son Bob Smith and his wife Anne, who were the most gracious and generous hosts during my many trips to Santa Barbara and Bloomfield Hills.

Like Sara, Bob and Anne, other Smith family members and friends were most open, supportive and helpful. Often, when I've explored a person's background, I've found stark contradictions between the public and private persona. But this wasn't so with Sara. Meeting childhood friends of Sara and Smithy—including Ben and Lil Chinitz; Irv and Jean Rosen; Milt and Annie Aptekar; Harold and Fran Weiss; Richard Lapin and Sara Levine; as well as Sara's cousin Phyllis Clinton, her niece and nephew, Marvin and Dorie Shwedel, and many others—only deepened my understanding of her kindness and character and provided a larger window into the jubilant life that Sara and Smithy led as they built their dream. (As Sara says, "Why not laugh? That's what life is about!")

I want to thank Bob Smith for his skillful editing, feedback and involvement throughout this process. I will miss working with him! Thanks, also, to architectural historian Fred Bidigare; to Bruce Brooks Pfeiffer, director of the Frank Lloyd Wright archives, and to Jordan

Gruzen, of Gruzen Samton Architects in New York City, for their professional input and guidance. I also very much appreciated Mary Palmer, who gave me another perspective on life inside a Frank Lloyd Wright home—this one looking out over a hillside apple orchard in Ann Arbor, Michigan.

There are many others to whom I am grateful. These include: Jane Shipley, who transcribed all my interviews with humor and insight; Maria LoBiondo, who conducted valuable research; Scott Wolf at the Getty Center, who tracked down correspondence between Frank Lloyd Wright and Melvyn Maxwell Smith; Howard Greenfeld and Alice Watterson, who edited this manuscript, and Leigh Bienen, whose encouragement was invaluable. Last but not least, I want to thank the Melvyn Maxwell and Sara Smith Foundation for its support of this book.

ABOUT THE AUTHOR

KATHRYN WATTERSON writes about a wide variety of topics, ranging from America's teenagers to modern medical practices to the plight of prisoners in the criminal justice system. She has received many awards for her writing, and her short stories, essays and articles have been published in a variety of national journals, magazines and newspapers. Her books, three of which have been chosen by the *New York Times* as Notable Books of the Year, include *Not by the Sword* (which won a 1996 Christopher Award); *You Must Be Dreaming* (basis of the NBC movie, "Betrayal of Trust"); *Growing Into Love* and *Women in Prison: Inside the Concrete Womb* (basis of the ABC documentary, "Women in Prison"). She teaches writing at Princeton University and frequently gives readings and workshops at colleges and universities around the country.

DESIGNED AND PRINTED AT
THE STINEHOUR PRESS
LUNENBURG, VERMONT

BOUND BY ACME BOOKBINDING
CHARLESTOWN, MASSACHUSETTS